THIS IS ME

KATIE PRICE

THIS IS ME

The High Life. The Dark Times. The Full Story

First published in the UK by John Blake Publishing
An imprint of The Zaffre Publishing Group
A Bonnier Books UK company
4th Floor, Victoria House
Bloomsbury Square,
London, WC1B 4DA

Owned by Bonnier Books
Sveavägen 56, Stockholm, Sweden

www.facebook.com/johnblakebooks
twitter.com/jblakebooks

Hardback – 9781789467796
Trade Paperback – 9781789467802
Ebook – 9781789467819
Audio – 9781789467826

A CIP catalogue of this book is available from the British Library.

Designed by Envy Design Ltd

Printed and bound in Great Britain by Clays Ltd, Elcograf S.p.A.

1 3 5 7 9 10 8 6 4 2

John Blake Publishing is an imprint of Bonnier Books UK
www.bonnierbooks.co.uk

To my family

CONTENTS

INTRODUCTION
30 YEARS IN SHOWBIZ

'I'M DONE ASKING WHY THEY KEEP DOING IT. NOW I'M GOING TO START ASKING WHY I KEEP ALLOWING IT.'

Anon

There is one thing that you should know about me before you continue reading this – I am unapologetically honest. I am someone who has been working in the show business industry for 30 years, and I am someone who has changed the game when it comes to being a celebrity. There is no one like me, who has survived as long as I have, that has created the headlines I have by not doing anything other than living my life. I am a woman of contradictions, which is why I think people can't put a label on me and why I find it very hard to describe my personality.

So what you are about to read is completely different

to anything you have already read. This is not an A–Z story about what's happened to me since my last book – because, believe me, in that time you couldn't even begin to imagine some of the stuff that I have dealt with. (And I will keep dealing with everything that comes my way because I'm a survivor. Sadly it's taken me longer to realise that than it should). One of my best friends Kerry Katona made me laugh the other day in one of her voice notes, after I had shared with her something toxic that was happening in my life and all the stuff I was dealing with. I think she summed it up perfectly:

'Kate, it's. . . [pause] your life, it's so, so bad, it's fascinating. Steven fucking Spielberg couldn't write this shit!'

She has a point.

You will notice as you read this book that the focus changes as I write. I started off writing about my experiences over the past 30 years in this industry, but the events of the last five years have overshadowed a lot of what was due to be a more reflective memoir. Which is why it's 'Which is why it ends with 'To Be Continued.' I don't want to sell you short, I believe you bought this book because you want to know the truth about what has been happening to me, and I believe you deserve to learn the truth rather than be spun a web of lies from the media. So you'll see that my book, though reflective of my whole life, will also be punctuated with the very real drama I am dealing with in my life at the moment.

I was 17 years old when I first stepped into this industry. Seventeen! I was a baby. I am now 46 years old and I'm still going. I know I am a rarity because how many people have lived what I have lived through and are still here to tell the tale? I am rare because I am real and a lot of people don't like that. From the moment I stepped in front of the camera I knew what I wanted, but a lot of people mistook that strength as me being 'difficult' or 'a diva'. And it spiralled from there.

I had this weird habit of being 'myself' everywhere I went and that's why not everyone liked me. I wasn't ashamed that I wanted big boobs and that I made money from getting my top off. God, how I wish I could go back to those simple days, the days when it was just about being paid for a job, for getting my top off and that was it. You'd have your photo taken, you'd pose for the camera and then you were done. Now I reckon if you Google my name – go on, do it – you'll see a list of different stories about me that will be a load of bollocks because they always are. Why is my life so fascinating to so many people? I honestly couldn't tell you.

I am a unique case, I get that. You will never find anyone like me. There might be people in the industry who have done similar things, but there is only one me.

Name someone else that can hold a candle to what I have created in the past 30 years in this industry. I have worked in every area of Planet Showbiz that exists – reality shows, talk shows, adverts, modelling, writing, creating, endorsing and selling. I've fulfilled a promise that I made when I was younger – to be famous. Nowadays, you get these massive influencers but what skills do they actually have apart from promoting themselves on social media? Seriously? That's all they can do. And guess what? I can do that too. I have evolved, and I will continue to evolve on whatever platform that's relevant, and I will continue on this show business journey knowing there is only one me. As I like to say, there's only one Pricey!

Maybe one day, eventually, I would like to work out of the spotlight. I would probably be a good mentor or motivational speaker or therapist. Everything I've gone through would quite likely help me to help others, because I really have lived and breathed the most traumatic events that can get thrown at one human being.

Every day I am tarnished either by stories that are written about me or because I've posted a photo and people have jumped to all sorts of conclusions. I live with embarrassment all the time and yet I go out every day – with all of that in the background – and I show up for work. I put on a suit of protective armour when I leave the house because I have a job to do. And people don't work if

I don't show up. They can't meet deadlines or can't record shows. It's not like an office job where there is another Kate ready to take up the slack if I have a sick day. There is only one me and it's exhausting.

People see me walking down the street and they'll be thinking, 'oh, here comes the drug addict or the alcoholic' or 'there's that awful woman who crashed her car drink driving.' But no one knows the reasons why those things happened. When I crashed, the police officer who was first on the scene was more interested in posting a photo of my crash on Twitter than helping me.

And you know why that is? Because instead of helping Katie Price, people like to expose Katie Price. When people do something, it's normally for a reason – even driving a car drunk – (more on that later) and yet people forget that with me. No one says to me, 'Are you OK? Do you need help? Do you want to talk?' They see my behaviour as something that is just 'bad'. They put me down because of things they have read or seen or heard. No one says, 'Do you know what? We can help you through this'. Everyone has an opinion on me but very few people's opinions are based on fact, instead they are based on what stories they've read about me that day.

The refreshing thing is that when people do meet me, they tell me how different I am and how shocked they are. It's like they are expecting some pantomime villain.

Instead I'm just normal, and I love it when people realise that, I love it when people see me and they do a double take. What? No horns? What? You're not walking around naked? What? You're not drunk? I am sat here writing this in my trackie bottoms and my hoody, with a cup of tea, slime all over the table because Bunny is into that (and it gets everywhere!) with Frog, my cat, on my lap. The children are at school. My horses are in the stables and my mum is here because she's not well and I want to be able to look after her for a bit.

But those sorts of things don't make stories. Instead there will most probably be a story online about me looking pregnant because I posted a photo with my belly out that someone has decided looks swollen. I'm judged that quickly and that decisively. The journalist will be writing a story on my 'baby dreams come true' before I've finished drinking this cup of tea.

It's a very weird world I live in. Unless you are in it and live and breathe it, people just don't believe it.

Which is the reason I have written this book. I have lived 30 years in an industry that probably gives you a shelf life of no more than ten, and this book is dedicated to the lessons I have learnt in that time, and the lessons I am still to learn from the people I have invited into my life. I have seen a lot, lived a lot and been hurt a lot. I have cried a lot, laughed a lot and have got married more than I should have. But I have survived it all and I will keep going. There's going to be no big revelation that my time in the spotlight is over (sorry, everyone), I'm not done by any means. I wake up with a small, but very real fire in my belly every single day. A desire to keep achieving anything I put my mind to because I love my job, I love what I do. I love that I have been successful for far longer than a lot of people will give me credit for. I love that I have pissed off certain people along the way but I also hate that I have let the wrong people take advantage of me. I love that no one can dictate who I am or put a label on me. I love that I am still a glamour model – I have been for 30 years – but now it's not on Page 3 of *The Sun*, it's for my OnlyFans website. I love that I am paid good money to work and I enjoy what I do, but I hate the way that I am written about as if I'm a 'product', not a person.

I hope that as you read about all the things that have happened to me, it will shed some light on the more damaging, hurtful and upsetting stories you have seen about me.

Headlines sell. Photos sell. Negative stories that are fabricated sell even faster, which create even more stories that are spun to create yet more and then suddenly, fiction and lies become reality, and people believe what they read online and in newspapers and in magazines.

I have actually lost count of the number of times that I

meet people out and about and they say how lovely I am, or how friendly I am. It's done with complete and utter disbelief; they are questioning our encounter because of the lies and stories that have been spewed out about me. I don't blame them. I tell them, 'Yeah, I am nice!' and we have a little laugh and that's it. Tomorrow they will probably go online and read a story along the lines of: 'Kate lands on her face as boobs have finally fallen foul of gravity just as she is being carted off by the police because she's been caught trying to ram into one of her exes while illegally driving an uninsured car, which is also carrying in it her new 23 pedigree dogs that she won't look after.' Reader, this has not happened.

I don't want to give you the wrong impression though. I am not making light of a situation that has plagued me for years. This is no laughing matter. You'll read more on this in a later chapter where I write an open letter to the press. There were lots of things I wanted to say to them over the years, and this seemed like an ideal opportunity.

This isn't just a book about my life in showbiz for the past three decades, it's a survival manual. It's lessons I've learnt, regrets I've had and situations I've negotiated during my time in the spotlight. And while a lot of my book is very firmly cemented in the past, the past few years have brought me more pain and heartache than I care to admit. It's fair to say that recently I have overcome situations that would break a normal person, that would absolutely crush the heart and soul out of them. But I want to set the record straight and share what's been happening to me in the same way I want to share truths and memories and stories that have happened to me over the many years you've known me.

Margaret Atwood once said: 'In the end, we will all become stories,' and so I am hoping that maybe people will remember my story, in my own words. I know I'm not for everyone but I have lost the ability to worry or care about that. I just think it's time that I settle some scores, that I have my say and that things are revealed that have long been hidden behind fake headlines. It's time for the truth and the truth is, I am someone who doesn't come along twice.

Would I change anything? Who am I kidding?!

This is me.

CHAPTER 1

REGRETS

> ## 'THERE IS NO FORCE MORE POWERFUL THAN A WOMAN DETERMINED TO RISE.'
> *Unknown*

A chapter on regrets is probably a strange place to start but I am in a reflective mood and having been in the business so long, it's a question I am asked quite frequently. 'Do you have any regrets, Kate?' Or 'Do you regret marrying (insert name here)?' Or 'Do you regret your 500th boob job?'

So, I thought I'd start here and see where it takes me. I think my first reaction is always; 'No, I don't have any regrets.' You can't change the past, so why would you regret anything? Where does it get you? But then I thought about it some more and realised it's probably a bit trickier to answer truthfully.

Regrets are a funny thing. On the one hand, I get that

you can regret something you've done. Or someone you've been with, or a situation you've been in. But often regrets are woven with elements of success and pride.

Do I regret running the London Marathon in 2009 after I had just lost my baby at 16 weeks? Yes, I do. It was dangerous and my body was not able to cope with the overwhelming trauma it was under while I was trying to force it to get me to 26.2 miles. It hadn't even been 24 hours and my mind was all over the place.

I was bleeding during the race and my knee was giving me agony. And then you have all the emotional pain that goes with that, all the people I thought I couldn't let down, and so I had to put on the bravest face I could muster and carry on. Because that's what I do.

Not long after that, Pete and I split up. I so, so regret not speaking up more when the media started playing us off against each other. You could buy *Team Kate* or *Team Pete* t-shirts and hats. People made a fortune from a devastating time in my life. There was no 'team', it wasn't a game. It was a really sad situation, it was a marriage break-up and yet it was treated with mockery and amusement by the press, and, sadly, also by people that I trusted, who saw me at breaking point and, despite that, continued over and over again to keep pushing me down.

(I'll probably regret saying this stuff later on, but I've got to an age where I think to myself, 'Fuck it'. I need to plainly and clearly tell you all how certain events have affected me. This is very much my story to tell and my feelings so yeah, 'Fuck it'.)

For so many years, stuff has been said about me from that time that were hurtful lies. People lapped it up, and I was easily put into the bad guy category because I continued to work and earn money and didn't sit around sobbing that my marriage was over – and that's because I love my job and I love being in front of the camera. (And oh, if I could go right back to the beginning of the Page 3 days and the *Loaded* mags shoots and the *FHM* spreads, I would. Life was so simple back then, life was easy – you did a job, you got paid, it was done).

But after Pete, the tide turned against me and people who knew me saw me at breaking point from all the pressure. There was no let-up from that point. There didn't seem to be anything positive that was written about me; it was just easier to make me out to be a villain.

But I feel I've gone off on a bit of a tangent here. I was talking about regrets, and the Marathon. . ..

So yes, in answer to whether, in 30 years in this industry I have regrets, I do. I do regret putting my body through a gruelling marathon, but I won't ever regret raising all the money we did for charity and for awareness of Harvey's condition. We ended up buying a minibus for the school with the money I raised. And that's how

I justify a lot of things that have happened to me; there are a number of regretful scenarios that hold both positive and negative aspects.

I definitely, definitely regret some of the men I have been in relationships with but ultimately, they have made me who I am today. I think if I am being honest, I regret letting myself be treated the way I did by men. I know I am a good mother. I won't stop fighting for my children. My children are everything to me and I regret not stopping this witch-hunt before it began. But more on that later.

I can't help the way I am. Again, I make no apology for that. I am honest and I will tell people how it is and believe me, that's got me into trouble over the years. But the problem with that is that, right now, I am going through the toughest time I have ever been through and fighting every day to make sure my children are OK and yet I am being judged by people who have read God knows what in the papers, magazines or online.

'Oh, that Katie Price? Isn't she awful! Isn't she always drunk and getting her tits out? She must be a bad mother.' And do you know what? I don't blame them. I don't blame that they have read stuff about me and formed an opinion. We all do it, don't we? You must have read countless stories about me over the years and rolled your eyes in disgust. But you have to remember, this is my life. And in my life, whatever I do, it ends up being played out in the public eye because I sell magazines, I fill a space online, I create debate.

I regret that people see me as something completely different to who I am, but that often leads to some of my happiest moments, when I meet people and they are like, 'oh, you're actually quite nice. You're normal.' Yes! I am!

I am a woman who has survived in an industry that is meant to destroy you. And there were occasions when it nearly did, when I nearly let it. So that's another regret, I suppose, that I didn't seek help, in the right way, with the right people. But more on that later – my therapy and my journey through darkness is one that I hope will help a lot of people.

One of my biggest regrets is that I seem to have lost the female solidarity that I built up when I first had children and was a working mum, trying my best in a difficult situation. I know there was a huge group of women who supported me, who got what I was trying to do, who enjoyed working – like I do – and enjoyed being a mother, and who have also been hurt by men or situations in their lives.

The key difference between us though is that my life is played out in the press and therefore twisted and manipulated to create a false narrative that has no bearing on my real life. You should see my life on a normal day. My house is noisy, it's chaotic, it's a house full of children and pets and people coming and going all the time. But my children are happy and they are looked after and they are loved. And I bet there are mums out there who are the same, who will be thinking, 'well, my house isn't exactly spotless', or 'is it Wine O'Clock yet?', or, 'is it too early to put the children to bed because I'm exhausted?', or, 'wouldn't it be nice to have some adult time once in a while?'

Am I right? You all can think it, hell, you can say it! You can make it a fucking post on social media and you'll have everyone come out and say, 'Yep, I hear you' or 'Gin being poured as we speak.' And I bet you don't get judged.

But me? I don't get to say that because as soon as I do, I get labelled: I'm a drunk, I'm a bad mum and I have a revolving front door of men coming in and out all the time.

Motherhood is hard yet, I'd bet if you say you are struggling, I am sure there will be people lining up, trying to help you. If I struggle, it's just another story in the paper about how awful I am. And that does get to you after a while. Sometimes it's hard to keep quiet.

But I often do keep quiet, and some of the biggest regrets I have in my life are things that I didn't say, that were left unsaid for one reason or another. I regret that I didn't see any of the messages that my friend and reality TV star, Nikki Grahame, left for me in 2021 when I was in a London hospital after breaking my feet. I had no idea she was on the floor above me, on the Anorexic ward, reaching out to me and asking me to come up and see her. But I never saw the messages as I wasn't in the right frame of mind to check my phone like I normally do. She must have thought I was ignoring her, when I wasn't. She died not long after that, and that's hard to live with because I am always there for my friends if they need me. But I never got to tell her that, that I wasn't ignoring her – I just didn't see the messages.

I also regret that I never got to talk to Caroline Flack before she died. She was working with a mutual friend in America and had messaged me because she was being hounded by the press and wanted advice on how to deal with them. A lot of the stuff they were writing about her was hurtful and not true and she was upset. She knew I was no stranger to that sort of publicity and had been dealing with negative press for years. But she wasn't used to it, she was fragile and had built a successful career on being a professional and popular primetime TV presenter who everyone liked and respected. She wanted to meet up so we could have a proper conversation about it, and we agreed that when she was back from the US we'd get together. But we never got to have that catch-up because she committed suicide only a few weeks later. I have nothing more to say on that other than what a complete waste of a beautiful life. It did take me a while to process that she was gone but I knew from her messages just how hard she was finding the press intrusion. I'm not saying that, had we met up and had a chat, anything would have changed. I know our situations were very different and I have probably become immune to things that can break other people very easily and very quickly, but I do think I would have been a good person to talk to. I have a lot of empathy and even though it might not have made any difference whatsoever, I would have tried. And I regret that I never got the chance to try.

I recently watched the Amy Winehouse film and it affected me more than I thought it would. I could see everything she went through in terms of my own life and the way the cameras would follow me and be in my face as I walked up the road. To have them constantly after you, in front of you, next to you. To have that fear that every time you went out someone is always watching. I know what it's like to have controlling people around you, making sure you only reveal certain things at certain times or act in a certain way. 'Don't hold hands! Save it for the photoshoot!' or 'Don't kiss now, wait for the interview!' The control to create a certain image has been pretty relentless throughout my entire career.

I've been told never to watch the Caroline Flack or Britney Spears documentaries because their lives are so similar to mine. I've been told not to, to protect my own mental well-being, but honestly, I imagine what they'd show me about what those poor women went through is not going to shock me in the same way that it might shock you because it's a reality I know very well.

* * *

It might seem odd to say this but one of the biggest regrets I've had in my 30 years in the business is Eurovision. I've spoken about this before, this isn't something new, but fuck me, what was I thinking? I still remember it clearly – being in that studio, in my pink jumpsuit, performing for the chance to be our Eurovision entry in 2005. I hated the song, I hated the costume but I'd been told if I took part, I would get a Sony recording deal out of it. I couldn't sing it then and I couldn't sing it now if I tried. I was seven months pregnant too so I'm sure that's a big part of why I didn't win. That said, Javine beat me by only 1 per cent of the vote. It was all such a shit show and I was mocked hideously afterwards. I suppose I could try and turn this regret into a positive because as I didn't win, I therefore didn't go on to represent the UK and get nul points in front of the whole world. Although I think Javine maybe got 18 points in total and came second to last, so not the worst. But where is she now? Perhaps it was a good thing I didn't get that gig. But yes, that is one of my biggest regrets and no matter how hard I try, I can't turn it into a positive.

Do I regret any of my boob jobs? If I had a pound for every time someone asked me that! The answer is no, I don't. I am the biggest I have ever been at the moment. I am 2500cc and that's the biggest I will ever go. I know 2500cc doesn't make a lot of sense to most people but that's me. I will probably want to go smaller before I've finished writing this book because I like to change things. Or maybe not. The only surgery I regret having is liposuction before I had my first boob job. It's a wonder that I ever had anything done to my body ever again after having that because it was fucking painful. And I'm not sure why I had it done. I was so young and tiny but it was a bit of a gimmick at the time, wasn't it? Everyone seemed to like the idea of having the fat sucked out of them. I only had it because I couldn't be bothered to go to the gym. As I was quite skinny I'm not sure I should have even gone through with it. All I remember is that my legs were black and blue and they started oozing when I got in the bath. Oh my god, the pain was absolutely bloody awful. I can't remember how much it cost – it would have been a lot more than a gym membership that's for sure! Although you'll be reading that and wincing and yet, I'm still sat here, thinking 'I need more lipo. . . my arms are a bit flabby, maybe I'll have more'. It's just who I am, and hopefully you'll understand why that is after reading this book. The liposuction and having my nose done are my surgery regrets. I liked my nose, I didn't even want it done, but when I was in America the surgeons were putting me under for a boob job so they said they would do it at the same time. It was just another thing to do, kill two birds as it were and so I said yes. I do miss my old nose, though. If I had it in a cupboard, I'd probably get it back out every now and again and wear it. Ha! But I don't spend a lot of time worrying about that; you can't. What's done is done. I don't have any major words of wisdom when it comes to surgery if that's what you're waiting for. Sorry. I don't want to be a surgical role model for anyone, I do what I do for me and me alone. I wouldn't say to people to have or not have surgery (although I do seem to get lots of people telling me what I should and shouldn't do!) as it's such a personal choice. I know the reasons for me having it, which I'll talk about more in another chapter.

The only thing I would say is that lots of people I know who have had boobs jobs have regretted not going bigger the very first time. It's like when you get a haircut, you only take a little bit off at first because you can take more off later. Well, with a boob job, people often wish they had gone bigger the first time so they wouldn't have to have another operation. When I took my implants out completely after I was in *Big Brother* in 2015, I thought my boobs would look disgusting and wrinkly and empty, like empty tea bags. . . but they surprised me. They looked alright. That said, would I ever go back to not having anything? Never. I know I spoke about it at the time being a reset, and even though my boobs didn't look like wrinkly old tea bags, I never want to go back to being flat-chested. When I look at the early photos of me in my modelling days I think I look rank. Sad, isn't it? People tell me how beautiful I looked but all I think is, 'How I ever got a modelling deal and got onto Page 3 from looking like that I have no idea!'

Thinking back to my early days of modelling – which were some of the best days of my life – it's also made me think of another major regret. I wish I knew then what I know now about copyrights on photos and having ownership of them. When I went out to America to be in *Playboy* in 2002, photos of me were plastered on the side of New York taxis advertising strip clubs. I had no say over where my photos were used back then and I wish I had been told, or worked out myself, that having ownership over your image is hugely important. I didn't agree to be on the side of a taxi advertising a strip club I had never visited. (Although, yes, I'll admit, I think it's pretty cool!) But it's been a lifetime of lessons from then on. I stayed in the Playboy Mansion for six weeks, and there was lots of things I saw in those days. There was so much action but, as I've said before, I didn't shag him – Hugh Hefner that is – that would be like shagging my grandad. No disrespect! But it was still a brilliant time – I was the first English girl doing *Playboy* after all so it was a big deal. I turned up at the mansion and I remember thinking, 'what the fuck?!' I was greeted by all these girls with their American accents, who seemed fascinated by my boobs. Me and Hef, we'd go out and tour around America, promoting that I was on the cover of *Playboy*. Oh my God, those days were just... I look back and think, did that all happen? Movie nights at the mansion when all the people would come over and watch films. Hugh was a nice guy. He thought I was wild. I suppose I was pretty different to everyone else; I didn't sleep my way up any ladder!

Jett's just come into the kitchen and asked me why I'm smiling to myself. He'd probably find it amusing to hear I was on the side of the famous yellow cabs. But then again probably not, I'm just mum to him. I want a cuddle and in typical 10-year-old boy fashion he doesn't want to be mauled by his mum and doesn't understand why I need to have these snuggles and kisses, but he indulges me and I love that. I can't be doing too badly as a mum, can I? I have stopped reacting to things on Instagram as I'm always in trouble after I do. I think a lot of my previous snipes or comments were due to my impulsiveness, my ADHD behaviours where I reacted without thinking or taking a moment. See, I am learning! Or I'm getting less reactive in my old age! Not that ageing worries me. Although I look at photos of Pamela Anderson and I think she looks rough now. She has a lovely smile but she's really changed since her heyday when she looked amazing.

She would probably say the same about me when I was younger. I looked totally different when I first became famous, when I first started dating Dane Bowers. . . he's a regret, I suppose, though I would love to see Dane again, and we did have a good time together, but then he cheated on me so it would never have worked. And no, before you ask, I don't regret all of my relationships. Each experience has made me who I am, but I can honestly say I'm not bothered about ever seeing or speaking to the others *ever* again. I call them my Mr Prices because, let's face it, some of them have only used me for my fame. To give them a platform. For five minutes in the limelight. We all know they were nobodies until they met me and I'm pretty sure that can't be disputed. . . Hang on, I can hear a drone over my house. Give me a moment.

Yep, there it is. It's a common occurrence unfortunately, the press flying drones over my house to get a glimpse of, well, I have no idea what they want a glimpse of to be honest. Maybe it's the cars that are parked here because I can't drive them anywhere since I lost my licence. I have been told I can have my licence back, but then the DVLA tell me that because people have emailed them to say that I'm unfit to drive, I need to get letters from my doctor's to prove I am. So I do. And I have done this four times. Can you imagine how embarrassing it is to keep going back to the doctor and saying, 'Please give me another note!' I can't help but think how easy it must be for people to ring up and report anyone, or am I just getting this level of attention because I'm an easy target? I might try it. . . Perhaps I could ask my sister if she wouldn't mind if I called up or emailed them about her driving and see what happens? Although she'll be pissed off if they do take away her licence. Perhaps I won't.

The drone is still hovering. I wonder if it's photos of the horses that reportedly run wild and that I don't look after they want? Or photos of my house. Everyone loves a story on the Mucky Mansion, don't they? Especially when they put what they think it's worth. I've had it valued and I can tell you the guide price you read in the papers is way off. I know what it's worth. I have that number in my head, and no one else knows. That's exactly how it is with everything else you read. I know I'm not skint, I know I'm not going to lose the house, I know how much I earn. You can think this, or that, or believe whatever you want to believe, because I know the truth. That's how I deal with it. Maybe I regret not suing the papers or magazines for making up stories in the past. Maybe I regret not kicking up a fuss every time a crap story was written about me. Although I'm not sure I'd be able to afford the legal team to undertake such a task. I'd be paying a lawyer a retainer every day!

I might go outside and flick the bird at the drone. I'm sure I won't regret that.

CHAPTER 2

MANIFESTING

'BEHIND EVERY STRONG WOMAN IS A STORY THAT GAVE HER NO OTHER CHOICE.'

Nakeia Homer

My sister Sophie bought me a book called *The Secret*. I still haven't read it yet, but I will. She told me it's about people who live their lives by manifesting what they want from the universe and that if you manifest positive vibes, good things will happen to you. To be honest, my first reaction was: 'what a fucking load of bollocks that is!' I manifest every fucking day that I want something good to happen but it never does! I try and put out on social media good stories, nice photos, fun memories or adventures with the children or horses and manifest positive reactions all the time. But it always backfires. Even my sister gets fed up when people start emailing her about stuff I have posted.

Sophie is my rock and my best friend – I don't know where I'd be without her (and all my family, actually: my brother, mum, dad. I'm where I am today because of them and their support). Sophie manages my social media accounts and, recently, she got an email complaining about a photo I shared of me and my horse Wallis which showed that he had a double bridle on. Of course I have a double bridle! I am an experienced rider, he is a dressage horse, I know what I am doing! Something so simple like a photo of me with Wallis turns into a witch-hunt by people who don't even know about tack or bridles or that horses have four legs and go neigh. 'I don't know what it is about you, Kate,' messaged Sophie when she got the email, 'people just seem to pick on everything.'

But then something clicked and I thought to myself that while I would love to have the universe on my side and for it to provide me with all the answers and all the happy endings, the only person who is going to turn this around is me. I am the only one who is going to make my life better, no one else. And it was time to take back control.

'Kate, you can do this. You are a survivor. Fuck everyone else,' I said to myself as I closed the front door and leant against it. But I didn't have time to let it sink in. I had just got back from recording an episode of my podcast, *The Katie Price Show*, to find a huge lorry on my driveway and my cleaner trying to organise two burly men dropping off all my possessions which had previously been seized. Only, they don't care that my stuff is important, or is valuable, or loved because it's of no value to them anymore, so they're just literally dumping it in the hallway, meaning there is stuff everywhere and one or two bits are actually broken. I spot a large signed and framed photo of me as Jordan and I do have to wonder why something like that was taken in the first place. Unless the bailiff was a fan.

I would probably laugh about all this if it wasn't so bloody ridiculous. 'Jesus, Kate, what is my life?' I said to myself as I picked up a neon light that had been dumped on top of boxes of shoes and dresses. There was literally stuff everywhere and it took a while to sort and put back. 'As if I haven't got enough to bloody do,' I said out loud to myself. 'I think I'll have a cup of tea first.'

I talk to myself a lot – I think this is a healthy thing, I'm sure other people do it. I speak out loud to myself if I need to focus on a task, or talk to myself if I ever need reminding that I am strong and I am capable. It helps me to understand and process information too and is probably the reason I have written so many books: saying stuff out loud to record my thoughts helps me understand a lot of situations better. Can anyone else relate to this?

I have survived when things have been tough, when

things have been thrown at me, things that I struggled to cope with, but I did it. The reason I am telling you this is that we all have triggers that can cause anxiety, or panic, or throw us off course. I recognise my triggers now and that's why I make sure I have coping mechanisms to bring me back on track.

I am stronger than I sometimes feel and I know I wouldn't be here if I wasn't. I expect you have faced situations in your life when you think to yourself, 'how will I ever survive?' or, 'how will I ever get through this crisis?', and then you do. And everyone is the same in that regard, aren't they? You deal with things you didn't think you're capable of – until you are tested.

Like being told your mum has a terminal lung disease. . .

I find it really hard to talk about my mum's illness and I won't lie, I've come back to this bit of the book time and time again because writing about it makes it real. And yes, it makes me sad. I was so upset when I found out, I couldn't stop crying. And I know people will find that surprising because they don't expect me to cry. I very rarely do. But this is my mum and I was devastated. I know I need to talk more about this because Mum's illness does need to be recognised but I am struggling. It's really tough to think about, losing your mum.

And it was a shock too. She'd had a cough for ages

and she couldn't get rid of it so she eventually went to the doctor's after a lot of nagging. Me and my sister went with her and the doctor said it could be one of three things. I can't remember what the other two things were but IPF, or Idiopathic Pulmonary Fibrosis, was one of them and I do remember the doctor saying that that would be very unlikely. And when he said that, well, we didn't really think about that option anymore. When the doctor asked Mum to blow into a tube, I tried to make a joke of it all and said, 'You're used to blowing on things, aren't you, Mum?!', trying to keep things lighthearted. I thought it was quite funny too.

But not long after that we got the diagnosis that Mum did have IPF and I was in complete shock. We all were, the whole family, we couldn't understand it. Mum was so fit, so active, so alive. She went to the gym every day and she didn't smoke. She was fuming when the doctor told her; she was so cross because she'd looked after herself all these years and yet she was suddenly faced with a terminal illness that had no cure. The best way to describe IPF is basically a scarring of the lungs and I think it's normally people who work with asbestos that get it. Mum had no idea where she got it from – though she reckons she might have got it when she went to India to work with kids via a charity a few years ago. It was on her bucket list to go to India and she stayed in a place where it was damp and dusty – it's the only thing we could think of but who knows?

I was so distraught and it was so hard for us all as a family to grasp the enormity of the situation because. . . well, I didn't want to lose my mum. Of course, I then went on Google (which is never a good idea) and the prognosis they gave for life expectancy was two to five years, but because we were told Mum's was so bad, I kept thinking, 'Oh, is she going to die soon? She won't last two years, she won't see Harvey turn 18 or Junior or Princess or Bunny or Jett grow up. . . ' It was the hardest thing I will ever have to deal with – and you know I have had a lot going on in my life but my constant has always been, and will always be, my mum. However much she moans at me or gets on my tits for not texting her enough.

'I'm going to tell you I love you every day, Mum,' I remember telling her this when we found out but then it got to the point where I didn't want to see her. That sounds awful but what I mean is, my mum has always been there for me; she has always been the bossiest, most active person you could meet and I didn't want to see her deteriorate into a shell of that strong woman and be all weak and feeble. That isn't who my mum is.

I think it hit me even more when she needed to have an oxygen tank because at that point I couldn't help thinking that if she catches a cold, if she gets a cough. . . that could be it. I would always have that in the back of my mind and yet at the same time I would try and be as normal as possible and remain positive and have a bit of banter because if I didn't, well, it could have all come apart. And that's not normal for me and my family anyway. We love a bit of banter, so if we had started acting differently it would mean that Mum's illness was really happening and I don't think any of us could deal with that for a while. So we'd make jokes about it. I'd call her a ghostbuster with her oxygen pack on or if she was heading outside, I'd shout, 'Hold up, Mum, you can't walk that far into the garden because of your oxygen' like she was on a lead or something. Or, 'Bloody hell, Mum, you're being lazy today, aren't you? Go and put the kettle on for us!'

Covid was bloody hard though – because she was so vulnerable, I couldn't see her for a lot of the time and never inside. We could only put our hands up to the window and pretend we were touching each other. It was hard but I know it was the right thing for Mum.

Dealing with death, it's hard for any family and I don't think there is anything that can prepare you for it because you don't know how you are going to react to it. We are a close family, we are incredibly open with each other – sometimes too much I guess, when Dad's walking round at home with his boxers on, scratching his knackers. I am, and have always been, the first one to rip the shit out of them all really. I'd tell Mum something like if she did a handstand, her boobs would be in the right place, that sort of thing. Dan, my brother, farted in her oxygen tube the other day too and she got so cross with him! Death is quite a serious talking point. It had no place in our family of banter and silliness.

What we soon realised, the more we talked about death as a family, was that everyone, every single one of us, at some point, was going to die. No one is going to live forever. When you confront that thought, and I mean, *really* confront it, you can turn this awful diagnosis around and think, Hang on, would I prefer for her to die suddenly in a car crash? Would I prefer it if she suddenly died in an accident and I never got a chance to say goodbye? Or is it nicer knowing that, this way, knowing she has a terminal illness means she will be able to spend time sharing memories and stories with us? Does that make sense? This way, we can talk about all the things she wants to tell us, all those special memories and stories. All that time realising how lucky we are and leaving us with memories to cherish.

Talking to other people in a similar situation, they have all said to us that it is a real chance to build memories, take pictures and live each day. And that's what we've done and are trying to do. Mum told me it was one of the reasons she wrote her own book, *The Last Word*, because she thought she was going to die before the book was released. She's planned her funeral too. She's even written a list of people that we have to tell aren't allowed to come! I was like, 'Fucking hell, Mum, you can't do that to me!', but I know I'll honour her wishes when the time comes.

I'm happy to say that Mum's getting stronger and stronger each day now and that's because, after five years of waiting, last year she was told they had found a lung donor for her and she would be able to have a lung transplant. It was such a hard time though because the doctors have since told us that she only had a few weeks left to live when she got a call at 8 a.m. to say a donor had been found and she had to get to hospital in the next three hours and they would operate straight away. I remember the day vividly – it was the day the Just Stop Oil protestors had caused chaos on the M25 and my parents were stuck, panicking, in the middle of the motorway chaos. Dad had to call an ambulance to meet them on the motorway so they could follow them and they could get to the hospital in time. Not that I knew any of this was happening at the time as I'd just flown to Thailand for a break. It was hard to leave Mum when she was so ill but she encouraged me to go, and I think I saw it as a chance to recharge my batteries just in case the worst did happen with her. I knew I'd need all the energy I could get to get through that.

I'd only just got there when my dad called and said, 'Just to let you know, your mum went down six hours ago for her lung op.' I was like, 'Fucking hell, what do you mean her lung op?' I had no idea they had found a donor – she didn't tell me or my sister. We were quite upset about that because it felt like we hadn't had the chance to say a proper goodbye to her in case she didn't survive the surgery and, of course, we both wanted that chance. We did both ask her about it a while later, about why she hadn't told us, and she just said she didn't want to upset us. We sort of understood that too because no one knows what they are going to do in these situations or how they will act, so you just do what you think is for the best.

After Dad rang of course I flew all the way back from Thailand. My mum had expressly wished that me and my sister stay away from the hospital initially while she was in recovery. Yet again, she was trying to protect us from being hurt and being sad and being upset, but we couldn't stay away.

We went to see her when she was in an induced coma and I remember thinking she looked like Violet Beauregarde from *Charlie & the Chocolate Factory*, you know, when she blew up like a blueberry! The person lying on the bed didn't look like my mum at all, who was all puffy and had all these wires attached to her. The nurses told me to sit and massage cream into her hands so that's what I did.

And I kept doing that, and everyone who came to visit did the same thing and massaged her hands.

From that moment on, we just took one day at a time and each day there was progress. There have been setbacks of course, jolts of realisation that even though she is still here with us she is still ill. I remember watching her the first time she tried to walk again after the operation and she looked like a really frail old woman. It was so hard to see my mum like that, so hard to see my rock being transformed into something so fragile. The steroids affected her kidneys too but now she is so strong. She's got better and better and she deals with everything that life throws at her.

I know I'm lucky that I've still got my mum. She's still there when I need her and she still moans at me every day, but if ever she's really winding me up, I know there will be a part of me that will say, 'Kate, you nearly lost her, you could still lose her'. Because that is the absolute worst thing in the world: the crashing, shouting, forceful, scream of reality that your mum is dying. But then, the banter continues. 'Come on, Mum, get up and make the tea! You've got a better lung than all of us now!' It's the way we all coped and I hold onto it to get me through those hard moments.

* * *

I'd love to go into schools, into colleges and talk to pupils about inner resilience and strength. What you know you are capable of, how anxiety and worry is a normal emotion. I would probably tell them about my phobia of needles. I am sure you all know I am scared of needles, I can't stand them, they give me major anxiety. But I will still have Botox injections in my face, I will have an anaesthetic for surgery and I continue to have tattoos all over my body. The fear is real, but I talk to myself about how I can overcome the emotion because I know deep down, my strength is greater than my fear.

It's the same with triggers. I used to see the word 'bankruptcy' and it would take me straight back to the Priory. I would see that word online and be triggered. It's the same with the name 'Kieran'. That name used to take me back to my breakdown in 2021 (did anyone realise this had happened to me?) and something goes funny in my belly and I will start to have a physical reaction. I find that there is a tightness in my heart and I will have a stabbing sensation in my stomach. These physical reactions require me to stop what I am doing and focus on letting the feeling pass. When I first displayed crippling anxiety, my doctors suggested that I hold some crushed ice in my hands, to focus on the cold sensation. It's a way of helping quiet your thoughts when they are racing through your body and, in a moment of panic, helps calm your over-stimulated body. Of course, that only works if you are at home – no one walks around with fucking ice cubes, do they?

Sometimes it does take a great deal of strength for me to remind myself that I'm OK. I have my house, I have my children, I have my family. The other thought that I will repeat to myself over and over again is, 'Nothing is the end of the world.' There's probably nothing I can't face that hasn't been thrown at me already. I will always earn more money, I will always fight for my children, and I will never let myself get into the dark place again. Bankruptcy doesn't hold the same fear now as I can see a way out of it. If material stuff is taken from me, I know I can earn it back. I will get into escorting if I need to, not to sleep with men, just for company. To be on their arm for a dinner date or something. I think I'd be good at that. My mum would tell me I need to work on my table manners first though. And by the way, that is a joke!

See, I try and turn even my worst situations into a positive. Every bad relationship I've tried to turn into a positive, but more on that later. There is a lot in life I am grateful for and continue to be grateful for. I have a roof over my head, money in my bank, five wonderful children and a career that has lasted three decades and too many memories to really appreciate. I know trolls, the media, will continue to put me down but I have learnt to live with that because my success is that I always come out the other side. My success is that they can't beat me.

While I know the trigger signs, other people still worry about me when they know there will be certain situations that may hurt me. For example, when I did panto last December, I was the Wicked Fairy in *Sleeping Beauty* at the M&S Bank Arena in Liverpool. I got a lot of bad press, stories saying I didn't look like I wanted to be there, how they had to cut ticket prices because people reported I was forgetting my lines. It was all bollocks. Audience members were filming me and ridiculing me. I am not sure what they were expecting. An award-winning stage actress? Did I ever say I was that? I must have missed the part when I announced that.

But the press obviously thought I was meant to be better than I was. I had to learn a full panto script, the dance moves, the songs – which I had never heard before – in just six days. So yes, I was bloody nervous and there were times I had ballsed up my lines because it was completely nerve-wracking. I'm only human. But I showed up every night, I didn't back down or pull out or give up, although I was absolutely knackered.

However, when my parents couldn't get hold of me during that time, they started bombarding me with worried messages.

'I hope you are OK', and then, 'Kate, are you OK?' I had

forgotten the impact that trauma causes on your loved ones. My dark moments weren't just times *I* had to deal with, the impact on my family was huge. But of course, I didn't realise that at the time. As soon as I realised that Mum was panicking, I messaged her back straight away. I didn't want her worrying about me with everything else she had on her plate.

'Mum, I'm fine. I'm rehearsing, I've been rehearsing all this time and I'm just trying to focus.'

And I would send my parents my rehearsal sheets so they could see where I was, and I'd say, 'You can see why I'm knackered!' But they are so scared by what has happened to me before. The problem is though, the care can become suffocating. Which I know sounds weird, because obviously you want people to care about you, but when they only think the worst every time, I find that makes me struggle more. It's like an extra pressure on me to have to comfort them and reassure them that I am OK when I am just trying to get on. I need to be given a chance sometimes. I want them to know I won't ever get in that dark place they imagine me going to ever again. Like driving a car when I'm over the limit.

And I am getting there slowly. Things are opening up again for me. And that's the great thing about manifesting – of saying to myself that good things are going to happen to me, and that good things are happening again – you bring a little positivity into one area of your life and it has a knock-on effect on other areas. There was quite a long time when I found people didn't want to work with me, but then one door opens and it's successful and so another door opens. People see you aren't the person they thought you were, and another door opens, and another, and now I am so busy, I am struggling to fit in all my work commitments. And working for me is so important, it's all I have ever known. I want to work, so it's a good place for me to be in. Of course, that can also have a negative effect as I have found myself turning down jobs because I don't physically have the time to do it all. I hate turning down jobs, it's not who I am. However, I know that looking after myself is more important than trying to do everything. I have my family and my children to think about.

Mentally taking care of myself is as important as my physical self-care. I get my nails done every week without fail. And I always make sure I have my hair done, or hair extensions or a blow-dry and colour on a regular basis. People might think it's indulgent or unnecessary, but I think doing little things for yourself makes you feel better. Maybe you treat yourself to a facial on a regular basis or a massage – it's the same idea. What makes you feel better about yourself you do, and that's why I have my nails and my hair and my eyelashes done. I don't know what it is about my nails in particular, but when they are done, I just feel good. I've always done it, I always will and I've got to the point now where I won't apologise for it and I don't care who thinks it's pathetic. The way I look at it, I would rather have that addiction than take drugs or alcohol to make myself feel good. I think my time in the Priory showed up the problems with how people are seen or want to be seen. In the Priory I met all sorts of people that had come in because they had lost face and their pride had been hurt, and pride to people like that is everything. It's cost them a mental breakdown because they couldn't keep up with the fancy lifestyle or the expensive cars or the private school fees or the designer clothes. That's what's quite funny about me if I think about it. I've never been one for fancy clothes labels, that's not who I am. I've always looked a bit of a chav! And pride has never got me into trouble either. There is no other side to me, what you see is what you get. I don't project an air of being a 'rich bitch' because, well, I earn a lot of money but I live in a home that everyone calls 'Mucky Mansion'!

I've just seen the time: it's 11.11 a.m. and I make a silent wish. I see double numbers all the time. It's meant to be lucky, isn't it? It's meant to be the universe's way of showing that a guardian angel is sending you a sign to follow your intuition. I like that. I like it especially at the moment because I have a lot of 'noise'.

I think noise is the best way to describe the stuff I am dealing with. It's noise in my head I can't escape from. I have this court case for my bankruptcy coming up and the newspapers are fixated on that and so it's become this one big noise in my head. In the past, noise like that used to be bad, something I couldn't cope with and would run away from. But now? I am so cold, so hardened to such things, now all I think is, 'Oh well, what can they do? I am still here, I've got my family, I've got my house, what can they do?' And so it goes back to being just noise again. I still have to acknowledge it, but I am so desensitised to it now that I just don't care.

When you don't care, in a way you take back some power. I am not scared of courts anymore, I'm not scared of getting a letter threatening court, I'm not scared of the police. I know there would be people who would go down a dark road dealing with what I have dealt with, people who might even commit suicide for being hounded in the way I have been. But again, I'm not scared. My response is now: 'go on then, do what you want, you won't hurt me. You can't hurt me and I won't ever get in that dark situation ever again. So take what you want. Or don't take it, or send me another letter. Or take me to court again. I don't care'.

After my time at the Priory, I now speak to my consultant there every two weeks which helps me because they write everything down, everything I say to them that I have been dealing with, and they document it and then they tell me that I am due something called 'Breathing Space', which basically means someone is on my side saying, 'Enough, now. She's had enough.' And rather than the excuse, 'I can't come to court today, I can't face it,' there is documented evidence, there are pages and pages of reports from the therapist which say, 'this woman is dealing with too much and she should be excused.' Because there is a breaking point to what people can deal with.

But I won't be beaten.

And here's something else too. I will always do what I want to do in my life, I won't have anyone tell me I can't. I have been manifesting singing opportunities and I am now being bombarded by people who want me to come and sing live, half-hour sets around the country. I absolutely love singing and I love singing live and I have gigs in Dubai booked in too. Singing my version of those big powerful ballads is like a dream come true. Manifesting your dreams does work, setting your intentions to the universe does work, and I tell you something else: never giving up on something you believe you can do works too. No matter what other shit is going on in your life, keeping a focus on one positive thing is the key.

I like to find the positive in every day, there is always

something to be grateful for or thankful about. I am reminded of this as I've just received a text from my friend Neil, inviting me to his daughter's first birthday. Neil was the one who saved my life when we were hijacked in South Africa when we were there filming for *My Crazy Life* in 2018 (more on that pivotal moment later on). He put himself in danger and he got knocked out and his eyesight hasn't been the same since. He saved us all. That invite, that's made me smile.

Finding the good in each day is important but so is giving back that positivity too. So I always try and make someone happy or make someone smile every day. It's not a grand gesture, it can be a nice compliment about something they are wearing or something they have done or going to do. It doesn't cost anything, does it? Giving someone a compliment is so simple, even if it's just saying to the people around me, 'thank you for your support today, I couldn't have done that without you.' I love the people around me, I love being at home, I love the chaos, I love the animals coming and going, the children in and out. It's taken a long time for me to trust again and to feel safe at home, but home is my safe space.

I've just seen another double number: time to make a wish. Or perhaps I should buy a lottery ticket? I did an advert for the National Lottery once and it was hilarious – you'll have to Google it – it was about eight years ago and they launched a new set of adverts with the hashtag #pleasenotthem. It was a complete tongue-in-cheek piss-take of myself and I loved it. I had absolutely no problem in having a laugh and being part of something that was obviously aimed at poking fun at annoying celebrities. The advert was about me wanting to launch KTTV, my own TV channel that runs 24/7 and sees me acting in all sorts of TV genres. I'm in every TV show imaginable: I'm a lawyer, a zombie, a DIY expert, a cowgirl, a cop. . . you name it. And the punchline is if I won the lottery, KTTV would become a reality. Hence the 'could you imagine how awful this would be?' hashtag vibe. Piers Morgan, Vinnie Jones, Noel Edmonds and Laurence Llewellyn-Bowen all had their own adverts in the campaign. I think at the time we were the most Marmite characters in the UK and I look back now and think how funny. But how sad too. Back then, I was a bit more respected as a person than I am now so it's ironic that while it was a complete piss-take about how people didn't want 'more' of me, it also, in a way, celebrated all the things that I was famous for.

Yes, I think I will buy a lottery ticket. I have a feeling I am going to win, I can't explain why. Lots of people say I have bad luck but the way I see it, I have the ability to turn it good. Like when I broke my feet on holiday falling off a wall in 2020, I made money on those stories so I figure if the world throws crap at you, smile and own it. Would a lottery win change me? I have already planned what I will do with it. I would be anonymous when I won and then I would go to court and I would let them batter the shit out of me about how bad I am, and then I would stand up, with a wad of cash in my hand and shout, 'Alright, you fuckers, how much do you want?! Here you go, stick it up your arse!' And I'd walk right out. Well, I would if I wasn't in contempt of court by then, but you know, this is my dream. Or I'd sit there all smug, let them put me down over and over and then stand up and throw money at them. 'Here you go!' I'd shout, 'sit on my middle finger 'cos I'm off to order a Rolls-Royce!'

You can tell I'm still so angry, can't you?

12.12 p.m. . . . time for a wish.

CHAPTER 3

BAILIFFS

'CHIN UP, TITS OUT, ONWARD.'

'Can I just ask you something?' said my mum to the bailiffs, which meant she was going to ask it anyway, 'Is being big part of the job specification? Are you only allowed to be bailiffs if you are huge? You are giants!'

'Oh, here we go. . .,' I sighed.

'Would you like a cup of tea? Boiled egg?' she continued.

'Mum! Please! I have offered them tea and something to eat. They are fine, they don't need you getting involved.'

'You don't have to be big, no,' said the biggest bailiff. 'In fact, one of my good mates who I work with is very small so no, it's not a job requirement.'

Satisfied, Mum went back to her breakfast, and I went back to trying to work out how surreal it was that there were two bailiffs (who did, it's fair, look like gladiators in their uniform) standing by my kitchen counter, one of them drinking tea from an old mug that had a topless photo of me with the name 'Jordan' on it. It was 9.30 a.m. on a random Tuesday morning but my life welcomes drama at every turn and that means I am often blindsided when I least expect it.

A few months ago this would have been the end of my world. I would have been inconsolable at the word 'bailiff' and the thought of strangers coming into my house and taking my things because I owed money would have triggered fear so deep within me, I would have found myself back in the Priory. But I didn't. And I am not.

The first time they came, it was pouring with rain and it took me a while to register who was at the door because they didn't look like policemen, but they wore the same blue body vests and had walkie talkies and body cameras. They came into my home and suddenly it didn't feel like a safe space anymore because it felt like it was being invaded by an enemy. Only this enemy you can't fight back against, this enemy you have to surrender to straight away.

And the invasions continued. They come in and they exert a physical presence that makes your heart beat really fast and your hands shake. Then they come again. And again. Never the same ones, always a different company. It gets to a point when they turn up, it's almost a jolly for them. Like they are trying their luck.

Then you become numb to it all. Suddenly, you have

lived through it and that hardens you, and you accept it again and again. The second or third time they came, one of them was a real bully. He presented me with a Dart charge, an unpaid fine for using the Dartford Crossing. It was for £899 and I was shocked.

'I don't have a car! I don't drive! I don't even have a driving licence!' I say, trying to make it clear there is no possible way I could be driving anywhere, let alone over the Dartford bloody Crossing.

But then he became aggressive. Bullying. He tried to intimidate me and said, 'We aren't taking anything, we know you can pay it.' He didn't show me any paperwork, any evidence, he just kept repeating that I owed him money and he wasn't leaving without £899.

I was so confused and shocked and was struggling to compute what he was telling me. . . Not only am I being asked to pay for something I didn't do and therefore had no knowledge of, I am being told he can take my stuff but he won't? I think my anger kicked in a little by that point as I say to him that I've seen the TV show, *Can't Pay, We'll Take It Away*, and I tell he can take what the fuck he likes.

And that pisses him off even more. So then he says he will arrest me.

I had no idea at the time whether they have the power to arrest me or not – who the fuck knows? – but I was so angry, I was shaking. But I wasn't going to be intimidated.

Now as I am writing this, I wonder how the stronger me would react? I would probably say something like, 'OK then, arrest me. That won't get you your money but go ahead.' I'd call their bluff.

Then there was another set of bailiffs turning up, another morning, coming into my house, telling me I owe £4,600 in Council Tax.

'No,' I tell them, 'I pay my Council Tax on a monthly basis, just like everyone else. I can show you.' And of course, they didn't believe me.

'We wouldn't have been sent here if you paid it,' they snarled.

'I have absolutely no idea why you have turned up,' I repeat.

'I know she pays it. I'm her PA, I have all the statements,' says my wonderful personal assistant, Jess.

'We have no evidence of her paying it so we are going to take goods and put locks on the door,' the evil little cretin continued.

I was astounded. 'But I pay it!'

It was only after seeing all my bank statements and direct debits that he left. No apology, just gone. But surely he would have had to check this sort of thing before he came? Surely they would have that sort of information before they start saying to people, 'you haven't paid this so we are taking your stuff now'?

Which makes me paranoid and nervous. Was he really a bailiff? Did I ask for ID? I believed him when he was at the door but then what? I am not a shouty person, I'm not an aggressive person, I don't do confrontations, I just need things explaining to me. I know full well I pay my Council Tax so now I was confused and getting angrier because who sent him and why? Do bailiffs try their luck? Is there a secret WhatsApp group that they are part of, where they say to each other, 'Katie Price is worth a try, we got a truck-load of goods from her last time we went,' followed by a laughing emoji or something?

I decide to ask the gladiators in my kitchen that morning about how it works because these guys were polite, they were explaining things to me and they were showing me evidence and so I needed to find out more. That's how my head works. There is often so much noise in my head that I need to hush it all while I deal with the problem in front of me. It's like needing to take a deep breath and clear your mind because you need to focus on one thing at a time. I needed to put my noise on mute so I could deal with the problem that was right in front of me that morning – which was another demand for money.

'Can you just explain what it is you are here for?' I asked, making sure that Princess's friend who was here with us that morning was recording everything on their phone.

'It's for unpaid Dart charges. You didn't pay for the Crossing, you didn't pay the fine within 28 days of receiving the PCN and we have therefore been instructed to come and collect £899.50.'

'But I had bailiffs here two weeks ago telling me I needed to pay Dart charges and so I paid it two weeks ago!' I say, absolutely flabbergasted. 'I had to pay this other bailiff £899 – the exact same amount!'

'This is for new tickets, which is why it's the same price. We have the dates and the tickets here, we can show you all the evidence so you know exactly what and when you are paying for.'

And at this point, those two poor gladiators standing drinking their tea get my life story. I won't stop until I have explained everything I have been through so I can try and make sense of it all.

'OK, look, I don't understand who sent you to me. I don't drive, I haven't got a car, I haven't got a licence. I am banned from driving and as you can see, I don't have any vehicles in a road-worthy condition to be able to drive down my drive – let alone to Essex. I had a very rude man come here before, asking for the exact same amount of money as you and I kept saying to take my stuff instead, and then a week later another man comes and tells me I haven't paid my Council Tax when I know I have, but he doesn't believe me and he doesn't do any checks or anything, he just keeps saying that I need to pay as that was why he was sent but he didn't tell me who sent him. And now I have you guys here, telling me I've got to pay the same amount as the first man who was here for the exact same reason...' I pause to take a breath. 'You can understand why my brain can't work out what the hell is going on!'

The two gladiators nod sympathetically.

'Kate doesn't even have a car to drive!' pipes up my mum. 'I don't understand why you people insist she has been driving and getting fines when she doesn't have anything to drive in the first place.'

'Yes, alright, Mum,' I say. 'Thank you, I've just told them that.'

'The thing is, I could drive your daughter's car right now and drive it over the Dartford Crossing and if that car was registered to your daughter, she would have to pay that fine.'

'That doesn't seem right to me,' says my mum.

'We get this a lot, people saying to us, "but I wasn't driving, I wasn't driving." And we have to say to them each time, "it doesn't really matter,"' said Gladiator 2, the slightly smaller one.

'OK, so we have the dates and the cars that drove over the Dartford Crossing and all the information you need. Did the other bailiffs show you when and what cars that was for?' continues Gladiator 1.

'No, they didn't show me nothing, just that I had to pay Dart charges.' My head feels like it is about to explode.

'OK,' says Gladiator 1, 'if you can find out the name of the other company who came, you should be able to find out what car and what dates it relates to. Dartford Crossings have three bailiff groups that work for them. They don't duplicate tickets so there is no way you are paying for the same charge twice, let me reassure you in that respect. They have to give a certain amount of tickets to each group, which is why you are seeing us today and you saw someone else from another bailiff group another day. Secondly, with Dart charges, you don't need to be driving the vehicle to incur a fine. It's not the same as getting a speeding ticket whereby whoever is driving the car is responsible for paying that fine. For Dart charges, like parking fines, it all comes down to who owns the vehicle.'

'Who is the registered keeper?' pipes up the smaller gladiator.

'Shit. . .' I say, as his words sink in.

'The car that has incurred these charges, as of last month, was still registered to you, which is why you have to pay,' says the biggest one again. He has a very calm and no-nonsense manner and it helps that I am being given information and being told what's happened rather than just demands for money. 'The dates for the Crossing were in July 2023.'

I'm still lost for words though, trying to work backwards to summer 2023 which seems like a blur to me now.

'Just bear with me,' I say, 'but you need to understand this. I lost my licence for two years, I did my community service, I did my online courses, I didn't come under a "high-risk" driver because I was only just over the limit when I crashed and I am due to get my licence back. But an anonymous person keeps ringing the DVLA to tell them I'm not fit to drive and so I have to get a form from my doctor and a form from my consultant and I have to send it off to the DVLA, and just when I think I might be able to get my licence again, someone from the DVLA tells me they have had another tip-off and they need me to send paperwork again. And this has happened to me four times! Some anonymous fucker has done this to me four times and it's just a joke.'

Both gladiators give a little nod in sympathy. Or maybe a nod to say 'bloody hell, woman, we don't need your life story!' But they are too polite to comment.

'Obviously you are querying the charges because you have had bailiffs before and it's not a pleasant situation, we do understand,' says Gladiator 2.

'I've been doing this for 15 years, I get it,' says Gladiator 1. 'You should have been provided with tickets or dates from the first bailiffs over the charges. We have all that information when we come on jobs, so people can see exactly why it is we are here.'

'You must get some right old arseholes,' says my mum before she starts coughing and coughing.

'Yes. . . sometimes. But it's the job we signed up for,' continues Gladiator 2.

'I'm sorry but I just. . . I still don't get it,' I say. 'It feels like I am being hounded at the moment by you guys – not you guys personally – but that anyone can come up to my front door and tell me they are a bailiff and tell me I need to give them money. And then when I pay it, or they take stuff and I think that's the end of it and it's gone away, another one shows up. It's all because of an ex who has registered God knows what cars in my name and is driving them, or getting someone to drive them, over the Dartford Crossing. You can see where I'm coming from, can't you?'

'Yes, of course, and the first thing I advise you to do when I give you the details of these cars is to make sure you take your name from the registration documents so that they are no longer in your name,' says Gladiator 1.

He proceeds to show me the crossings, the cars, the dates and it's all a bit of a blur to be honest. In my mind all I can think is that the car doesn't work. . . it's SORN. . . It's fucked.

'Do you want another cup of tea?' asks my mum after I have handed them my card details to pay the fine.

'No, thank you, we will get going now. But just to let you know you have, at this moment in time, three more crossing fines that haven't been paid and although they haven't been escalated to us yet, they are likely to be going to bailiffs if they don't get paid.'

'When are these ones for?' I ask, almost too numb to this whole scenario to really take it all in.

'It shows that these crossings were for August and September 2023. As I say, they aren't with us yet but they will be if they aren't paid,' says Gladiator 1.

Gladiator 2 has obviously seen my face. 'Look, it's very common. I get loads myself, we are on the road all the time. But you can challenge them and pay them within the time and then it's nothing. It won't ever have to get to this stage.'

'I'm just so desensitised to this all now, to be honest with you, bailiffs and court. I've got to a point where I am saying to myself, now what is there going to be?'

'Look, you can see on here, let me show you so you know the charges are for three crossings only,' says Gladiator 1.

'See no one ever shows me that,' I say, leaning over to see his screen. 'Fucking hell, that's a bit battered, isn't it?' He's showing me a tablet screen that looks like Harvey's had his hands on it and thrown it across the room. 'But it's still working, I wish Harvey's iPad's still worked after getting a bashing.'

'It's a bit shit but it does the job. My son is the same,' says Gladiator 2.

'Is he? I just wish I could get Harvey to stop smashing his up. As least your phone iPad thingy still works. Harvey smashes his and it breaks so easily and then we have to replace it with the exact same iPad. It can't be any different otherwise he kicks off. It has to be the same size, the same colour, the same version, completely the same.'

'Yep, exactly the same with my son,' says Gladiator 2, 'He's autistic too.'

'Is he? Does he talk? Is he strong? How old is he?' The poor man. I am so inquisitive when I meet people who are like me, who have autistic children, because I like to know all about them and what sort of things they do. 'Do you have that panic when you think the shop won't have the exact same one? I do. And I have to say to Harv, "Don't worry, we'll find it, Mummy will find it."'

'Best find it,' says Gladiator 2. 'I have the same problem.'

For a moment the atmosphere was just a little lighter because we were two people who were discussing a situation that not many people can relate to, but affects people from all walks of life. There was probably nothing else that me and Gladiator 2 had in common, but I think that by acknowledging and recognising that things are sometimes tough for us both, we understood each other a bit better.

'Right, that's all gone through,' says Gladiator 1, 'We'll get out of your hair now.'

The payment had been made and they were going. I was honest with them when I said that these visits were now so commonplace, I was desensitised to them.

'Don't forget to pay the tickets that are coming that aren't with us yet. Or challenge them.'

'Thank you,' I say, 'and thank you for being nice.'

'Yeah, we are nice bailiffs,' says Gladiator 1 as he leaves. 'But don't tell people that because we have our reputation to think of. Let's hope we don't see you again.'

And with that, they were gone.

'It wasn't just me, was it?' says my mum, 'They were bloody huge.'

'Yes, Mum,' I say, putting on the kettle and watching them drive away.

Five minutes later, there was another knock at the door. The next drama was about to unfold.

CHAPTER 4

DEAR COCAINE...

'I'M LOYAL TO THIS STREET, IT'S SIMPLY CALLED HURT.'
Song lyrics, 'Town of Sad', Anita

Dear cocaine,

You're not my friend.

You got hold of me at the wrong time.

How dare you?

You are affecting me and you are affecting my family.

You aren't letting me be the mum I want to be.

I can't be the mum I want to be because of you.

Fuck you. You will never be in my life again.

I hate you.

Kate.

In therapy, they encourage you to write a letter to someone or something that you need to say goodbye to. Or that you need to say something to.

I was never one to do drugs, it was never my thing. But then I became depressed. And I became so badly depressed that I couldn't get out of bed and I started self-medicating on cocaine because it blocked everything out.

Suddenly I didn't have to deal with anything because I couldn't think about anything. It was a coping mechanism that involved running away and the destination was a blissful period of nothingness. A place to forget, to not think about anything. Only you don't forget. You can't run away. And the problem grows. So you keep doing it. And you do more coke. And then you become dependent on not feeling anything. You become addicted to not feeling anything.

And this isn't a choice in a rational sense. I didn't choose to be anxious or depressed. I didn't choose to feel that way but circumstances in my life were out of control and I was doing what I had to do to survive. By switching off completely.

I was so badly depressed in early 2020, I couldn't get out of bed. I couldn't function as a person, as a mother, as anything that resembled a human being because I was self-medicating on cocaine because it gave me that sense of complete shut-down. Where no processing or thought was required, just a state of nothingness. It blocked everything out.

Coke came into my life and I welcomed it because it

helped me. Or I thought it helped me. It helped the me who wanted to hide away and not deal with anything, it helped the me who was depressed and not wanting to think. Now, I can see how controlling it was and I am shocked when I remember how dependent I became on it. Have you ever done something that you then look back on with such certainty that it couldn't be you because the 'you now' can't comprehend how the 'you then' could possibly be the same person. It's a bit like that for me, processing how I was then. Doing coke wasn't me, it wasn't who I was, and it shocked a lot of people. It still shocks me, to be honest. But I have survived and I have come out the other side. Self-medicating on coke is not the same as being an addict. An addiction is defined as 'a pattern of drug use that leads to clinically significant impairment or distress in an individual'. Self-medication is essentially 'a form of self-care in which a person seeks an effective remedy for a health concern'. I wasn't self-medicating because I wanted some sort of free-range intoxication, I was self-medicating on coke because it was the substance I chose to prescribe to myself. Because Kieran had brought it into my life and told me it would help me. I was never one to do coke and it shocked a lot of people around me who know me and couldn't understand my need to have this control.

The only good or the only positive I can take from being in such a dark place and coming out the other side is that you learn how to identify the patterns that set you off, the triggers, so you will never get in that place again. Triggers are a massive thing and I can't control when they come into my life but I can control how I react now. I never, ever want to be in that place again, which you might think is easy to say but not easy to keep but let me tell you, there is nothing easy about this.

On the days that the press are writing lies about me, that the bailiffs turn up at the door, that I have a court hearing to attend, that social workers visit my house. . . those are days that test my strength and resolve because the easiest thing would be to fall back and to block out and to remain oblivious again to my surroundings.

But I will never, ever be put in that situation again. I will never, ever put myself in that situation again. I have more strength and more power than that. This is the first time I have spoken about this to anyone other than my therapist, my family and my letter to Cocaine signing me off from it. It was the goodbye letter.

I am sharing this with you because there is a lot of stuff happening in my life right now that relates to how I was in the past because people are using my dark days against me and not that journey I have since taken to get back on track. When you are judged as 'an addict' it's somehow impossible to prove otherwise and I can't quite understand what else I need to do to prove it.

Why do I need to prove it? Well, that's a question that I'm not sure I can answer as so much is happening in my life that is tied up with all sorts of legalities. So I go on with my life as best as I can. If I'm not working, I am in my bed most evenings with a cup of tea watching *Married At First Sight Australia* or a film on Netflix. That's my downtime, my time to switch off.

I have been labelled an 'addict' and I will do anything in my power to try and change that perception, that I am not who they read I am in the papers – and I'll continue to do so. You couldn't make my life up.

* * *

I went to the Priory this week. I stopped writing this chapter and I went to see my therapist. He saw me at my absolute worst six years ago when I was first admitted and I see him on a regular basis. It helps bring some calm and clarity into my life so I think I'll leave the writing for today and do some manifesting instead. . .

CHAPTER 5

COMMUNICATION

'THE WOUND IS NOT MY FAULT BUT THE HEALING IS MY RESPONSIBILITY.'
Marianne Williamson

There is a poem that I was given in the Priory and it reads:

doves exist, dreamers, and dolls;
killers exist, and doves and doves;
days exist, days and death; and poems
exist; poems, days, death
early fall exists; every
detail exists; memory, memory's light
exist, and the future, the future exists.

When you are at the Priory, one of the activities they get you to do, especially if you are dealing with trauma, is to read through poems and song lyrics and underline words or phrases or even whole sections that mean something to you. The above were all lines that I had picked out and run my black pen across. It's weird looking back at it now because I remember being there and doing that as a different person, because it was before I had learnt a valuable lesson – communication. You have to communicate, even if it's not easy. Communication holds so much power, power to bring about that glimmer of hope that you'll find your way through whatever darkness you are living with. Slowly, things become more manageable if you can talk.

Let me explain it a bit more. In therapy, I learnt about this condition. It was called rumination and it's about a type of repetitive thinking that revolves around negative thoughts and feelings.

You might be able to relate to it if you think of it as a song. We all know that there can be songs we hear that get stuck in our heads and before you know it that song, or 'ear worm', can be slightly annoying, but it's not like it's a horrible experience. Rumination is a symptom that is found in both anxiety disorders and depression, and it's when negative thoughts loop around in our head continuously. It's a mental compulsion and is completely unobservable. These distressing thoughts, that are on repeat in your mind, can leave you exhausted and emotionally drained, and you can't see any ending, because when you ruminate bad thoughts, there is no completion to that circle. I sat there and listened to the therapist explain it to me, listening to his voice describe exactly what was going on in my head. It was like he could see all my thoughts swirling around in a circular motion – the same way in a cartoon when a character bangs their heads, you can see little stars circle around above their heads in a continuous loop.

I knew, before the therapy session was over, that I was guilty of rumination. I was guilty of ruminating all the bad things that were happening to me. They would be on a running track loop in my head and I couldn't see a way out. For some people, rumination can be replaying a scenario over and over again, or having the same thought and not being able to break away from it. For others, like me, the cycle is just a swirling of all the bad things that were happening in my life that I couldn't find a way of dealing with. The cycle in my brain moved from bills I had to pay to people who wanted something from me, to bailiffs, to the media, to going to court and then full circle again. It went round and round in my brain. This is the point of it; it seems like there is no escape from the endless cycle and thinking about all those things on a loop becomes an obsession and you can't stop it. I tried really hard but I just couldn't break away from all the non-stop negativity.

This is the point where the therapist steps in and persuades you to write down everything that was on your spin cycle. It's a way of seeing it in black and white. Then they ask you to try to prioritise these negative thoughts. When you make your list it's an attempt to gain back a bit of power over ones you can see can be dealt with more easily versus those that take up the most amount of space and energy. So I did exactly as I was asked and wrote my list, but there was absolutely no way of prioritising what was more important, or what needed dealing with first, as everything felt so huge and powerful in my head.

They were all big to me, and they all wanted my attention. They were all shouting at the same volume, and it was like this constant background noise that no one else could hear, and I couldn't turn it down or mute it or ignore it or switch channels.

To me, those thoughts represented everyone who was on my case, everyone who wanted to see me fail, to put me down, to see me suffer and to hurt me.

So then what happens is that you start ignoring people as an act of self-preservation. You want to shut out everyone and you start ignoring messages because you don't know how to answer people. Then you don't answer people because you don't want to anymore, and eventually you don't answer people because you've reached a point where you can't.

In the group sessions I did in the Priory, they mix you up with people who have come in for various reasons. You have people who are struggling with addiction to drugs or alcohol or gambling, and then you have people who are battling depression and then people like me suffering from Severe Trauma rehabilitation and Post-traumatic Stress Disorder. All different people, all suffering different addictions or traumas, but you suddenly find a connection. You see that other people think the same way you do, that they have worries and fears that are just like yours and it helps to know, on some level, that you aren't alone. It makes things a bit more bearable, that whatever you are suffering from, it's not just happening to you. You might be the only one dealing with the stuff happening in your life, but you aren't the only one dealing with problems and you aren't being judged for them.

And it's in those moments that you realise that there is a way out, that there is a switch inside of you that can turn down the noise. Or there is a voice inside you that you couldn't hear before because you only heard the negative and it says, 'OK, enough now. You've got to do what you've got to do. Time to wake up.'

And then slowly, with that little voice, with that bit of communication with yourself, you start to find a way out of the cycle of negativity. That type of communication is key. If you don't communicate, you will find yourself down a very dark road and the noises in your head will get louder and louder. And it's those noises and those people, that you don't want to communicate with, who are the ones you need to face.

I avoided communication to protect myself. It was a self-sabotaging act because all I was actually doing was making the voices that I was trying to ignore shout even louder and louder. I knew that I needed to communicate with the people who were saying to me, 'you've got to make this payment, you've got this to pay, don't ignore, don't ignore,' because before you know it, the problem gets bigger and bigger, and you start getting letters with red warnings, then you get court letters and all of a sudden, that noise in your head is deafening. I didn't realise at the time but all that happens when you stop communicating with people is that you get more scared and you do more damage than you ever realise by trying to hide away.

So you open the gate of communication, and you start by saying openly and unapologetically, something like, 'I'm in the Priory, I am having a breakdown', and it slowly eases off.

And then you communicate more and more. And you feel better when you say to people, 'I'm struggling at the moment, I can't do this right now.' But you explain what you can do, you explain what you are capable of at that given moment and you explain that you are trying your best. Because ultimately, that is all you can do. You can only be honest with people and the more you communicate with someone, the more the noise eases off because you have opened that door.

And slowly, this huge mountain of feelings that you felt you were up against – everything the world is throwing at you – becomes less and less scary.

You find that people start to understand you more, and you realise you are still alive, so what can they really do to you?

And lastly, you start to communicate with yourself again, and this is where I am now. I talk to myself all the time because I know that it reassures me. 'Kate, what else can they do to you? What else can they say about you? You have explained the situation, things will get better.'

Communicating with people allows you to regain a bit of power in situations you didn't think you could control and that turns negativity into positivity. You feel better for offloading because people understand you more, especially when you have held your hands up and said, 'I need help, but I'm trying.'

Communicating in magazine interviews was for many, many years my way of getting my voice heard. It was also, sadly, a way for people to twist my words and so now I stay well clear. My form of communication is now with

TV reality shows that I control because I am the star of them and I can control exactly what I say. They are still edited, of course, but you know me well enough by now to know there is no script and no agenda.

I will only do podcasts now too. Doing a podcast with my sister has given me the chance to react to some of the press stories directly and so people get the truth from my own mouth. I love doing them with Soph – she and I talk about everything and anything, and it's given me a freedom of communication that I've never had before. It's so liberating because people can hear my point of view about stories that are online and I can explain right away that they are a load of crap. I love our banter, I love how there is no limit or censorship – which I had for years and years with magazine and TV interviews. 'Don't mention this, make sure you don't say that'– the control always came from other people and was always held over me. But no more!

Communication. . . It's made me think about how I have communicated these past 30 years. I have been labelled all sorts of things in my time: 'brash, vulgar, opinionated, blunt, a liar.' I have found that I have leapt in at the deep end more times than I probably care to count and have been in trouble for giving my honest opinion or for messages I have posted. I am so careful not to 'react' anymore. There was a time when those people who were my triggers would spark a reaction in me and I would go on Instagram and react. To stop that, I got to the point that if I wanted to send a message, I would write it but not send it. Or I would write it out and I would wait ten seconds and I would think, 'it's not worth it.' And now, I don't even bother. I have learnt not to bite back anymore. Well. . . sometimes.

CHAPTER 6

TRAUMA

can still remember his ginger freckles. I can see them as clear as day, the intensity of them, sprawling over his face. It gave me something to fixate on, I suppose. And I don't need to close my eyes to see his bald head with wisps of ginger hair. He was a complete stranger who was in my life for no more than a few minutes 39 years ago, and yet I can vividly see him like it was yesterday. And that's because this man, this monster, sexually assaulted me when I was seven years old. This man who licked me. Who made me lick the end of his knob while white stuff came out of it.

I was *seven.*

Afterwards, he pointed up to a block of flats in the distance. 'I'm going to go back there and get you your pound and an ice cream.'

He was so calm and his voice echoes in my head as I write this. I had gone to the park with my mum and some friends, and there was a bush that formed part of a cut through to the park. It was the middle of the day, the park was full of children's excited laughter and the sound of playing. My mum was only a feet away on a bench but I was a world away in a nightmare of sexual exploitation.

I wanted to go back to this park, to St Ann's Well in Hove, to find the bush before I wrote this chapter, but I couldn't bring myself to do it in the end. Has it changed? I don't know. It was fairly ordinary by park standards, children had been using it years before me, and they have continued to use it years after it was the scene of my sexual assault. It's still being used now: endless streams of children being pushed on the swings, going down the slide, parents watching the adventures on the scattered wooden benches. It's a park to every other single person and child who visits, but to me it's a crime scene, a place of horror. It's the place where everything in my life changed. My need to revisit it probably comes from both wanting to get some closure and to get some understanding of what was the beginning of a series of traumatic events that I have since endured. If I do ever go at some point in the future, I think I would be disappointed if there wasn't some sort of plaque, some sort of permanent marker that says, 'Kate Price was sexually assaulted here'. Not because of some desire to have this part of my life recognised by visitors, but because it was such a significant, life-changing event in my childhood. Because if I ever went back, I would want to scream, 'it was here, it was right here.'

Using the cut-through to the park was something I had done many times before and many kids used it. In fact, the man was interrupted by another boy and girl coming through the bush. I think it was that boy and girl who called the police because not long afterwards, when the man had gone, the police came into the bush where I was still standing and started asking me questions. They took my knickers.

This incident, this event in my life, is something that I have never put behind me but it's something that I didn't think had affected me as much as it had until I talked about it on *Piers Morgan Life Stories*. Actually I couldn't talk about it on the show as I was crying and I very rarely cry. I don't know why I cried. It's a mystery to me, almost as much as how an adult could do something so horrific to a child. I wonder what made me cry when I was asked about it on a TV show and yet I can talk about it so matter-of-factly all the time?

To my knowledge, I never cried about what happened to me when I was a child, but in that moment, under the studio lights, with my family all watching, I did. Perhaps it does affect me, my first episode of abuse at the hands of a man.

It was also from that moment that I felt men were always looking at me. Like I was being watched by men everywhere I went. I suppose having your innocence shattered from a young age does that to you. Or maybe I felt that men were looking at me because they knew what had happened, that perhaps I wore an invisible sign around my head that no one else could see except other predators. A man tried to grab me and bundle me into his car many years later too. It had been in the papers that this had been happening and that women should be aware and as soon as I heard the car slow down next to me, I sensed trouble. He didn't manage to get me, I ran and called the police straight away.

I have been a victim of sexual assault on two more occasions. The second was with a celebrity, but though I want that acknowledged, I'm not going to be naming them here. My third time happened when I was in South Africa and I will talk more about that in another chapter. I wanted to focus on relationships in this chapter and the way that abuse – be it physical, emotional or mental – has been a thread running through some of my relationships with men. It's taken probably until now to see the pattern more clearly, because when you meet a new man or start a new relationship, you want to see the best in that person, you want to believe that this might be different to the others, that they might change your whole perspective on men. But then you end up being disappointed all over again.

* * *

'You've got a fucking great guy by your side and you're going to have me at Christmas and it doesn't get better than that, my lovely. You are made of some fucking steel shit, honestly. Love you loads.'

Kerry Katona made me chuckle with the voice note she sent me. I would be crying if I didn't try and find some parts of this whole, sad situation funny, and say what you want about Kerry, she's been in my life for years and we always have a laugh when we're together. We are doing panto this Christmas, we're going to be in Cinderella as the two ugly sisters and I can't wait!

And it's nice to have something to look forward to, isn't it? Because Kerry is absolutely right.

I've spoken about the men in my life in lots of my other books and podcasts, but I think when you look at them in hindsight and not when you are living it, you come away with a different perspective. It's very hard when you're in the situation to be anything but emotional because you are so involved but now I think, 'Shit! How have I let all these men control me and abuse me and use me for so many years? Like, how has it happened?' The problem is they don't come into my life as evil and controlling, they come in as nice guys but then their true colours come out.

Do I think that all men cheat? No, I know there are good men out there. I still believe in love and I see good in people.

And it's so different writing about it now because I feel that I have taken back some of power over them in a weird way. They have all shaped who I am but none of them have broken me. Some of them have come close and have tried – and continue to try. I know I can't change what has happened to me, but I will talk about it until I am blue in the face if it helps other women know that men who control or abuse or manipulate them is nothing to be ashamed of, that it's not their fault. That's the first thing I would say to women or men who've been in abusive relationships (because it's not always women who are the victims): 'It's not your fault.' For so long you believe that you are the ones that have caused them to behave like this. They make their own decisions and those decisions aren't your responsibility.

We might as well do a run-through of some of them

now. They've played a part in my 30 years in showbiz – and they have all come into my life through work or through people I have known in the industry. But at some point or another, some of them have controlled or abused me or dominated me or cheated on me. (Sorry to all the men out there who aren't horrible and who aren't abusers or cheaters. I know all men aren't as bad as some of the ones I've had in my life.) Here they are, in no particular order of importance or severity, but in the order of them entering and leaving my life after my first encounter with a sexual predator when I was seven years old:

A paedophile called Kees Quant, although that wasn't his real name, that's what he told Mum and me that he was called. I was modelling for Joe Blogg jeans in Churchill Square in Brighton and he was one of the photographers. He told my mum that I would make it big as a model and he was so convincing that it didn't seem a problem when he asked for me to be dropped at his house on a number of occasions to model and then Mum would collect me later. He lived in Kingston in Newhaven and he lived with his parents but he had a set-up in one of the rooms. So my mum, and sometimes my nan, used to drop me off and the first thing he would ask when I went into his little 'studio' room was would I like one of his pineapple milkshakes. He offered me one every time I went in, and every time I said 'no', because I didn't like the look of it.

I don't know why. I was 13 years old and he made me pose in suspenders and all sorts of adult stuff, making me stick my tongue out too. One day when Mum dropped me off, there was another woman in the room and he wanted me to wear a white shirt with no underwear underneath. He said the shirt would be wet too: 'We'll make the water warm so you won't be cold.' He was acting like it was so normal but there was no way I was doing it and I left. I spent the rest of the time sat outside waiting for my mum to collect me. That was the last I saw of him, though many, many years later, I am sure I saw him walk past me on the street.

Not long after the wet shirt incident we had a knock at the door and a child protection officer came in and explained that the photographer – who went by 11 different names and who had 11 different bank accounts – apparently, he had photos of me on his walls in his cell and they told me that the drink I had refused had probably been drugged too.

It was a strange scenario to get my head round. I knew there was something off about him but at the same time he was so normal-looking, it caused a lot of confusion in my brain. It was a harsh lesson in trust but I know I was lucky despite being exploited and vulnerable. I didn't realise that I would meet a lot more characters like him. . .

About three years later, I met a guy who I shared stables with who had just come out of prison. He was 25 years old and I lost my virginity to him. He was very bad news and he would cut up my clothes, push me about and Mum would have to pick me up when I ran out of his house and called her from a phone box with no clothes on. He kicked me in the belly when I was 16 years old and was pregnant and I lost the baby. He always tried to control me and whenever I went in the car with him, he told me to always face straight ahead. I couldn't look around or to the side because he thought I would be looking at other men, even if there were no other people on the pavements we passed: my eyes had to be straight in front.

Then I met Gary. Everyone called him a warthog 'cos he had a wart on his bollock. He lived with his mum and I would stay over with him all the time, but he would leave me there and say, 'I'll call you after football then we'll go out.' It would get to 9 p.m. and I wouldn't have heard anything, and I would be waiting and waiting. He would be out in the clubs by that point. Escape in Brighton was his favourite and he wouldn't get back until 5 a.m. I would be so upset that he never called or came to get me but it was all his way of stopping me going out so he could get with other girls. Towards the end of our relationship, he got a bit handy with me, pushing me about. Nice guy, eh?

Then I met Warren from the TV show, *Gladiators*. I won't go into that one too much but he admitted he was horrible to me and that the relationship was toxic.

Then I met Dane Bowers, and I was with him for a while but he cheated on me too. I met him at a film premiere. I was on my way home from a photoshoot when my friend called me and said to come meet her at the cinema. (I think it was a Will Smith film premiere but I can't remember which one.) I found out he was cheating on me when he went to do a gig in Ibiza. Hand on heart, he was the love of my life. We were living together and I loved him but when I found out I was pregnant, I aborted the baby. I know it was the right decision at the time. I loved him but he was a serial cheater. Truthfully, I wish I never aborted his baby. But I did.

Then I was with Dwight. He cheated on me, he lied, but I became pregnant and I had Harvey. And Harvey is the best thing to have happened to me.

Then I met Scott Sullivan before I went in the *Jungle*. Am I missing anyone? Oh yes, the Gareth Gates thing but that was quick. You don't need to know all about that other than he lost his virginity to me. I caught Scott with a stripper on the sofa before I went into the *Jungle* so it was all over by that point.

And then I met Pete.

I thought it was love, and when we split, it was like

I was in a state of mourning – not just for the future but my past.

Then I met Leo and he was very good-looking, but he ended up annoying me in every possible way so that was over pretty quick. He always made noises in bed or when he ate and he would wait for me to entertain him and in the end I just got annoyed.

Then I met Kieran and it ended up being a horrific relationship. The betrayal was such that you wouldn't wish it on your worst enemy.

Then I was with Kris Boyson but he cheated on me and coming off the back of Kieran, I was devastated. So that damaged me too.

Then I met Carl. I broke both my feet a month into our relationship and he essentially became my carer. We met during Covid, which had its own difficulties, but then he couldn't cope with the person that I was when the restrictions eased. He saw a totally different me and it went downhill from there.

I've since found out that he would secretly record me and some of my conversations, and he then put them out on social media. I changed the way I looked and I changed the way I dressed for him. Then I would see him looking at girls on Instagram and all the girls he cheated on me with were girls that looked just like me when I first met him. So he wanted that look but he didn't want me to look like that. It was a head-fuck. He wasn't very good with the kids either, except Harvey – but I think that's just because he liked the good press he got from it. He was one of the best-looking guys I ever went out with and when we first got together I genuinely saw a future with him but deep down, I didn't trust him. He started putting me down in front of the kids and then he wouldn't let me go anywhere. It was an on/off relationship too and when we had break-ups, he would go with someone else so I did too, but he didn't like me doing that – he wanted me to wait for him. I look back and can't believe I kept taking him back.

Writing this now, I think that what is so sad about my relationship with Carl is that I genuinely loved him. I think deep down, I will always have a bit of that love. Despite everything, I genuinely thought I would marry him and have his kids. I thought we could have been perfect together. If it wasn't for the way he was with me, I think I would have still been with him. Maybe he'll change if he reads this and realise that he can change, maybe that will help when he's with someone else. Because it's sad. And we could have had such a perfect ending if he wasn't the way he was.

* * *

I can honestly say men have been the death of me, especially with how quickly I run/jump/hurl myself into relationships. Until I went to the Priory, I didn't know about boundaries and so I jumped from one man to another because I was needy and vulnerable.

I obviously picked the men that say the right things and do the right things, and I ended up thinking they must be 'the one' without actually investing time to really get to know them. I would marry them or get engaged to them and move in with them so quickly. Going to the Priory has stopped all that. It's made a huge impact on everything.

Of course, I regret most of my men choices but the way I look at it now, it's made me the person I am. They've cost me money and heartache, and some have damaged my mental health. When I look back, there is a similarity between them all. A pattern.

My job was a major problem for some of them, they didn't like me doing the glamour stuff. Which makes me laugh because they all knew what I did before they met me! When they get to know me, they see I'm very down to earth and don't love myself at all, but my job is still something I absolutely love doing because I am an exhibitionist.

Would I go for different types of men? None of my men look the same but my preference is for a man who is well-groomed and who looks after his appearance. I have never had a man who has swept me off my feet, who says, 'Right, I'm taking you away for the weekend, pack a bag and let's go!'

I have never had men that have made decisions because I am always the one to do it. It's always me.

I also think people are intimidated by me but when they are with me, I seem to turn them into controlling, possessive people. Is this my curse?

Bunny has just come in for a cuddle and I look at her and she is so like me. She's wearing her jodhpurs, her hair is all curly and flyaway and she's spent the morning mucking out her horse and giving her cuddles and kisses. And that makes me so happy.

CHAPTER 7

GETTING BEHIND THE WHEEL

> '**YEAH, SHE FELL.**
> **SHE GOT DISTRACTED, LOST**
> **HER DIRECTION,**
> **MADE SOME MISTAKES,**
> **BROKE SOME PROMISES,**
> **FORGOT WHO SHE WAS. . .**
> **BUT SHE GOT UP.**'
>
> *3 A.M. Thoughts*

The banging noises in the cell are the most comforting. I lie here listening to the almost rhythmical knocks and bangs and I close my eyes and think of Harvey. These are like his noises – the banging sounds he makes when he's throwing something or breaking something – and so I find them quite soothing. So I lie on this hard, unforgiving bed in the police cell, and think of Harv. It gives me a huge sense of calm on what has been a terrifying night. I have nothing else to do but wait. No phone to distract me, no people trying to get my attention, just me. The police officer has just brought me in a hot chocolate, which was nice but the food was rank. They offer you something to eat when you are in a police cell and I chose the cottage pie but it was disgusting. It was so rank even I couldn't eat it and I have been in the jungle and eaten fucking kangaroo testicles. I don't make a fuss though, I had a bit then left it and I went back to lying down. Back to the calm, to my thoughts. How did I get here? The past two weeks replay in my mind as if on fast-forward and I try and make sense of all that has happened and how I now find myself in a police cell in the middle of the night.

* * *

'I was punched. . . then I ran.' This was the front page of *The Sun*, I'm sure you all saw it and remember it. But all that really happened was that I had had an argument with Carl. We were sat watching *Love Island* and he saw a message on my phone about Kris, my previous boyfriend. There was absolutely nothing in it but because of that day, my whole life imploded. But it turned out to be the turning point I needed in my life.

Carl wasn't allowed to speak to me for two weeks after they arrested him. He hadn't punched me, I know that, but he wasn't allowed near me. When I did manage to speak to him I told him I knew he hadn't done anything.

I had actually gone to the Priory after everything happened. I needed to speak to my therapist about everything and after listening, they wanted me to come in and stay for a while. I decided against it. I was filming my reality show *Mucky Mansion* and I wanted to continue with that. This wasn't because I wanted to be distracted by the filming, I was enjoying doing the show and I didn't want to let anyone down by not carrying on. Filming while your head is completely fucked and all over the place is probably not the best decision but there you go. It was a struggle and there were so many things that I found fucking frustrating about it, like when they wanted me to bring a garden table into my kitchen to make it look like I didn't have anything in there. They needed it to look mucky although everyone who comes here says it's anything but. They also wanted me sitting on a beanbag when I had a fucking sofa. I don't know why. Well, I do, but it's annoying.

The night I drove the car, I was home on my own. Earlier in the evening I had some friends round for a few hours but they had left. One of them had some coke on them and, yes, I had a little bit of it, probably a couple of lines, it wasn't even a lot. I had some alcohol too. This wasn't normal, it wasn't me, but I think this build-up had been happening for a while and I didn't realise it yet but it was all coming to a head.

When my friends left, I was alone with no kids at home and needed some distraction. I had previously ordered loads of new school uniform for Bunny and Jett from Marks & Spencer and so I got that delivery out on my bed and started sorting the clothes into piles. I put a film on, I put my little heater on and I started going through everything and putting shirts and dresses onto little hangers while all the while in my head, on a constant loop was; 'I can't do this, I can't do this. . .'

And then Princess rang me. I could tell she was upset so I asked her what was wrong. My daughter was ringing to tell me she wasn't allowed to see me and my heart just broke.

My head was spinning. 'The social workers are on my case because of what had happened with Carl, I can't see Carl. What am I going to do? What am I going to do?' I was frantic and I know I wasn't thinking straight but all I knew was – at that moment – I needed to talk to someone. I needed to see my friend and I needed to go right that minute and I didn't care that it was 2 a.m., I didn't care about anything anymore. I left the house with my car keys and I drove.

My friend only lives in Henfield, which is a short distance from me, but because my head was fucked and I couldn't think straight, I couldn't find his place. I had been there so many times before, I knew exactly where it was but that night, my brain being in the mess it was, I couldn't find it. So I turned around to come home and that was when I crashed. My car overturned and that's all I can remember. 'I don't want to be here, I don't want to be here,' was apparently all I kept saying, according to Lee, the man who found me and helped me crawl out of the car.

Mum is still traumatised by it. Even now she will have a panic if she hasn't heard from me. Which means every morning I send her a voice note that says, 'Hi Mum, I'm awake, I'm fine.' I know I've scarred my family but at the time, when you feel like you are having a breakdown, you don't realise the damage you are doing to them or your friends because you can only focus on your problems. You are ill and in a dark situation, and you can't see a way out of it, which means you don't have the brain space to think about anyone else. It's only when you are better that you realise the impact that your trauma had on them, and because they love you, what's happened to you has also hugely affected them. I regularly see a therapist so I know I am doing the right things but my family will still worry and panic if they can't get hold of me. I think it will take them a long time to get over that. Which is why I make sure I message or I reply or I answer the phone. Dad came round last night. He brought me a chicken kebab and we had a chat, which was so nice. Although I didn't have the bread bit because I am going to the gym at the moment so I just had lots of shredded chicken and onion and garlic mayo. You won't be surprised to hear that JJ didn't want to come near me that night!

Straight after the car crash I was taken to hospital and I had to do a wee test and a breathalyser before I was taken to the police station. Mum had phoned a lawyer for me and from the police station I went to court the next morning, and then straight to the Priory. I didn't go home, I went straight there and I was in there for the next five weeks.

CHAPTER 8

THE LAST RESORT

> **'UNSTOPPABLE THEY CALLED HER BUT I SAW HER STOP MANY TIMES. I THINK IT WAS IN HER STOPPING THAT SHE FOUND HER POWER.'**
>
> *Donna Ashworth*

The last resort. That's what it was called in the Priory. A nicer way of saying 'suicide'. Well, not a nice way of saying it, but you know what I mean. The last resort meant that you had exhausted every other possible avenue available to you, that you had tried everything you could possibly do and you were now facing a final decision. The first time I went to the Priory, in 2018, I noticed that it didn't matter what brought people into that place, whatever their starting point, they go through the same steps to reach breaking point. Some people get there faster than others, for some it takes a while to reach but people get to the same point eventually. They all reach the last resort. And that was me, that was how I was feeling.

There are lots of moments I wanted to share with you about being in the Priory and therapy but the book is only so long and I can't fit it all in! The most important fact to remember is that I was diagnosed with severe Post-traumatic Stress Disorder (PTSD) and I went into the Priory for trauma rehabilitation. It wasn't just what was going on in my private life even though that was a lot to deal with – kidnap threats for ransoms; my husband cheating on me; I was starting my bankruptcy proceedings; had court cases; my horse and dog had both just been killed; the media were all on top of me. . . fucking hell, that's a lot isn't it? But something else had happened to me while I was filming my reality TV show with my family in South Africa. My reaction to the incident wasn't normal. Talking about what happened to me in such a blunt and matter-of-fact way wasn't normal and therapy helped me understand that.

Why did I continue filming after the hijack and sexual assault? Why? Because I thought I would lose my contract and I needed to work. I am always having to prove myself to others; I am always being told that I won't be able to do this, or I can't do that, or that I'm not good enough. So I kept working and kept trying to suppress everything that happened that night, but of course, that meant I never had time to draw a line under it. There was always another thing, and then another thing, and it got to the point that everything was building up on top of me and I just wanted out. I wanted out of this life. I tried to kill myself.

I tried to commit suicide. I still find it hard to talk about because it was six years ago. I will admit to wanting to take my own life but for now, that's enough. Perhaps I will talk about it more when I feel ready. Maybe in the next book. Maybe never.

Mental health still has such a stigma attached to it and I have no idea why. If you shut down and don't want to talk about it, people say you are cold and heartless. If you open up, you are too dramatic or too emotional. It's a battle I can't win and probably won't ever win, but I know what works for me. I will say this until I am blue in the face, and I tell other people who are dealing with stress or mounting pressure in their heads – tell someone. Talk. Communicate. You might not want to, but it will save your life. I tried to take my own life when I didn't think there was any other option. I didn't see another way out for me. I look back at my Priory notes now and I can see, my scrawls across the pages about not wanting to be alive. . .

I was in South Africa with Junior and Princess and a

crew filming for my ITV reality show. Actually, let me start this from the very beginning. . .

When I was 15 years old, I met my best friend, Neil Tawse. I really fancied him from the moment I first saw him, he was the hunk of the gym. And he was going out with a girl called Natasha, who ended up marrying Gary Lucy and having kids with him. As I said, I always fancied Neil but nothing ever happened. All these years on, we've remained friends. Actually, more than friends, we are best friends. We've never had sex and never had a one-night stand or got together, we are just really good friends! And it's funny because over the years, all the girlfriends Neil has had, none of them liked me because of our friendship. And over the years, all the relationships I've had, none of them have liked Neil either. It's like they've been threatened by our close friendship. When I crashed my car the night I did, it was Neil I was going to see.

So we've been friends through everything and I've lost count of the number of people who have thought that we'd get together but we remain absolute best friends and I owe him my life. He's from South Africa originally, which is why I agreed to do the reality show with ITV1. As Neil was from there I said he could show us a bit of his native country; I wanted to show Junior and Princess the country too and we arranged a safari.

Before we went, Neil and the director of the show

discussed the route and discussed what was going to happen, what filming they would do to get all the best footage and all of that. It was all mapped out and everyone was happy. But when we got there, it turned out that a different route had been agreed. I don't know why or what really happened, but I know that Neil was concerned about the safety as he knew the area so well. Looking back, I think we probably didn't have enough security either – I'd heard a few things about places that were unsafe but it only really hit home when we landed there. I remember feeling generally unsafe. And with a film crew in tow, you do draw attention to yourselves! We weren't just a normal family taking a trip, we had cameras following us so of course we would be looked at and talked about and people might tip off other people. . .

Anyway, we did the safari and afterwards the director wanted to do a longer, different route home. I can't remember where we were heading, but we were at a café having something to eat and a guy with all our luggage said he would leave first and get going. He was South African and said he'd take the first car with all our stuff and we just had to follow on. So then it was just two cars, a car with the film crew and our car which had Neil, me, Junior and Princess in it. Neil was driving. The camera crew all got in the first car and we followed behind. We had walkie talkies with us and after a while I had to radio to say that Junior needed a wee and we needed to stop. We were on a deserted type of road and there weren't a lot of options of a toilet so we just decided to stop at the side of the road. Junior got out and I remember seeing him on top of this bank as I got out too. I decided I needed a wee so I thought I'd squat by the side of the car too. Princess was behind me and there was a female member of the film crew out of the car with us too, she was standing with Princess. I heard Junior shout, 'Oh, Mum, look over here, imagine if I jumped down over that bit,' pointing to the edge of the bank he was on, and I think I said something like, 'Oh, Junior!'. The next thing I know there was so much shouting around me, something loud like the word 'Casa, casa, get in the fucking car, car. . .' and I couldn't quite understand but the shouts were so loud and so harsh and so sudden. We all just sort of stood in stunned silence but we could see six black guys getting out of a car and they were all shouting at us. And I think it took a minute or two for my brain to process what the hell was happening but I remember instinctively grabbing the kids and running back to the car.

My memory is a bit shot with it all, if I'm honest. It all happened so quickly but at the time it seemed like it went on forever and it felt so surreal too. I kept thinking, *Is this happening? Is this actually happening? Am I dreaming this?*

So my memory jumps a bit too. I remember bits and bobs, I remember being in the car and we'd shut all the doors. Neil was in our car and all the guys were in the first car, staying put. I could make out two of the men, who I now know to be hijackers, trying to get into the car in front while the rest of them were around our car. I remember trying to shout out of the window to the car in front to come and help us because we were surrounded. But no one did. No one could. And so we just sat there. It was terrifying – the kids were screaming and I kept saying to them, 'Don't worry, you're fine, you're fine, everything will be OK. . .' but I was absolutely petrified. I genuinely thought that was it, we were all going to die. The lady crew member then got in the back with Junior and Princess and all the shouting and the screaming makes the noise all seem one big blur. The next few minutes are all a horrible blur too. They managed to get in my door, their hands were just all over me, and in me and down in my trousers. I just kept saying, 'Get off me, get off me, I've got nothing, get off me.' But they took everything, all the jewellery I had, my rings and my watch. I've still not got any of that back.

I remember shutting the car door then and I saw some of the men try to go to the back of the car so I screamed bloody murder. I think I saw red and I saw that Princess's door wasn't shut but I knew I wouldn't let these men near my kids. . . and then all of a sudden Neil was in the car. . . no, he was out of the car. . . I'm sorry, my memory is all so jumbled! Next thing I remember is trying to find the keys to start the car and I had the keys but my hands were shaking so much, I couldn't get them in the ignition. It was like watching a film but it was happening to you and you can see your hands and you can see the keys and where they need to go but nothing was quite adding together. And then it was too late. . . the hijackers saw what I was doing and they quickly opened the door and snatched the keys off me. I always take a pillow with me and I remember putting it up to my head thinking they were going to shoot me, I was waiting for them to shoot me through the pillow. But I just wanted to protect my kids, I wanted to stop them getting to my kids. Neil got in the car then and all I could remember saying to him was, 'I haven't got them, I haven't got them, I haven't got them.' Neil just looked at me and I can remember the look on his face. He got out of the car and said to the men, 'Right, come on then, if you fucking want it, have it!' And he started trying to beat them up but there was so many of them. They started beating Neil, it was horrible to see, but he was trying to fight back. He managed to wrestle the keys back off them and get in the car but then they whacked him, either with the butt of a gun or something else. It was brutal and suddenly there was blood everywhere.

Neil was knocked out and the screaming from the rest of us was deafening. The look of complete fear on their faces is a look I won't ever forget; when you see your children living a horror story and you can't stop it, you become haunted by it. And all the time I'm looking at them, I have a sense of 'we're dead. This is it now. We're all dead, we're all going to die' but the words that came out of my mouth were different and I heard myself looking at Junior and Princess in the eye and saying, 'You are OK, we'll be OK, everything will be fine.'

Then suddenly, as quickly as it all happened, it went completely silent. The men had gone. It was a bit like a zombie film after that. We got out of our cars in a state of shock, thinking, *what the hell is going on? What just happened? Where are they? Are they coming back?* And then the realisation hit that we had been given a chance to flee and to get help and so we ran to the road, trying to flag down a car. But no one stopped. There we were, trying to wave down cars, but because of the area we were in, no one would stop. They all knew not to stop on this road, it was too dangerous.

I started moving more and more into the road, the rush of adrenaline spurring me on. I didn't want to be ignored, I was determined to make a car stop and help us and, in the end, a family stopped. They could see I had my kids with me and they could see I wasn't a hijacker.

I remember begging with them to help us. I was like, 'Please, please help, he's hurt', pointing at Neil, whose face was absolutely pouring with blood. The family just looked at us and told us to call the police and I kept saying, 'We haven't got any phones, they've taken our phones, they've taken everything.'

The family said they saw the police just up the road so they turned around and dropped us back off. We had no keys to either vehicle now though so we were completely helpless, sat on our own at the side of the road, feeling like sitting ducks. And I know they probably weren't that long but it felt like the police took ages to come; it seemed like forever. And we were terrified that the hijackers were going to come back. But the police soon arrived and we were finally safe. We sat in the back of the police car and an ambulance arrived for Neil too. The police told us that we were incredibly lucky we didn't die. In fact, they said it was a miracle we hadn't been killed as they explained that the hijackers would have taken our keys, gone away and dumped everything they had taken and then come back and finished off the job. So basically, they'd come back to kill us and then nick our vehicles.

That was a thought that I didn't process at the time and I still find hard to compute.

The hijacking made the local news, not because of who I was but because we had been hijacked and we had survived. It turned out that the road we were on was a road that people knew you never got out of your car because it was so dangerous. If only we'd known that at the time!

Some of the film crew flew back the UK after it happened because they were so traumatised but all I remember thinking is, 'Do we fly home or do we carry on filming? I need to work.' Obviously, I was in shock. And I decided to stay and film, even though now, now I would have insisted on flying home in an instant. Neil's eye was fucked, he had stitches in his eye and to this day he can't see properly and has a scar.

We've all been affected by it. To this day Princess doesn't like going out in the car when it's dark. She still finds that situation hard.

I know we won't ever go to South Africa again either, nor the kids. It might sound awful but I start getting panicky if I ever see a black guy in a black hoody with an adidas sign on it. That image of that man will stay with me forever.

I phoned Kieran later that night. I was hoping he would fly out and be with us but he didn't. I didn't know then that he was already having an affair, but it was the beginning of the end for us. Obviously I had to tell Pete what was going on too so I rang him and explained everything, but that the kids were fine and we were going to stay.

I'm still angry about it all now to be honest, but Neil

put his life on the line for us and it's made our friendship stronger than ever.

Neil had arranged for us to stay with his friends for a few days after the hijacking, just to get our heads round what had happened in the safety of people he knew. ITV arranged extra security for us too, which helped us all feel much safer.

So we stayed in South Africa and spent a few days at this house, trying to decompress. I remember that, at one point, either the day after it happened or the following day, we had just had some food and I was in a onesie drinking wine. I remember that onesie vividly. All of a sudden, we heard this big 'bang' noise and quickly realised there had been a car accident right outside the house. I went into crisis mode. I started ordering people around, 'We've got to go and help! Right, you get blankets, you get something, come on, we've got to help!' and although it's all a bit of a jumble in my brain, I remember suddenly being outside in my onesie and pulling this guy out of his van, which he had crashed into a tree.

I tried checking him over, shouting out for others to call the ambulance while I put him in the recovery position. I went into autopilot, I think, and it wasn't until later that I thought, *we've just been hijacked, I've just saved a man's life, what the fuck else can go on??* My brain was going a bit, thinking about it all; there was so much that had happened, and I am struggling even now to process all the memories from it.

A couple of days after the car accident we agreed to carry on filming and the next adventure we agreed to do was swim with sharks. I mean, looking back now, swim with fucking sharks? What was I thinking?! And I remember we were in the car, travelling to the beach where we would join the boat that was to take us. We'd stopped at the traffic lights and we could see a police van in front of us. And then all of a sudden we saw a prisoner escape out of the back of this truck and start running up the road. All we could do was shout, 'Look, look, look!'. Like, we didn't trust our eyes at this point because, seriously?! We carried on just staring as police started chasing this guy. At some point, the lights must have gone green and we just carried on, like, *OK, another incident. We will process that all later with the others too.* That same journey I spotted a dead body just slumped over the side of the metal barriers on the road and we just drove past, like it was the most natural thing in the world to see. I think when you're confronted with things like this you see these things but you don't really *see* them – your brain doesn't process it. I think you just become immune to it all and this trip was quickly becoming a big blur of horror.

When we arrived at the meeting place on the beach, we started putting our wetsuits on before we watched the safety videos about what to do and what not to do in the water, what the experience would be like, what would happen and what fish we should see etc. And then the next thing I remember was that we were out on the boat and the water was so rough and to this day, I have no idea what we were doing. I can't tell you that I was excited, I think I was just going through the emotions. And we were on this boat being told about the cage they'll put you in, and that we could 'freestyle' swim with sharks. So, me and Neil being us, we decided that having been through what we had just gone through, we would just go straight into the water without anything between us and the sharks.

Junior and Princess wanted to freestyle too but I made them go in a cage. When the boat stopped in the middle of the water, it was still rocking because the water was so rough. I remember looking down into the water and there must have been about 30 fucking sharks just swimming around us, some of them bigger than the boat, some of them swimming under the boat.

I kept thinking, 'What the fuck am I doing? What the fuck am I doing?' and in the background there is this noise of the splashing of the sharks and talking of the people on the boat, telling us we'll be fine to swim with them as long as we stick to what we're told and that they had been doing this for a long time and the sharks wouldn't bother us. . . Chaos, right? It sounds it even as I write this but it was all part of the blur of the trip. The next thing I remember is that I am sat on the edge on this boat, thinking again, 'What the fuck?!' And then I see Princess and Junior in the cage and them being lowered into the water and before I can think or process or fully appreciate what I am doing, the adrenaline starts pumping and I was in the water too. And then there were just these fucking huge sharks that sort of tap you, that brush past you and their fins. . . when they swim under you can feel their fins brush right underneath you, like they are painting a line right down your body and it's so surreal. I am looking at the kids in the cage and I am looking at the sharks around me and there is too much to focus on.

Honestly, I am writing about this now and I can't for the life of me figure out what the fuck was going through my mind at this point. It's like I am looking back and watching a person that looks like me, like in a film and I'm shouting at the TV, 'why the fuck are you swimming with sharks?!'

And what the fuck would the people on the boats have done if the sharks did decide to take a bite out of us? But at the time you get carried away with it all.

What was I thinking? There is no way I would ever do that again. Maybe at that point, having been in a situation when I was convinced I was going to die and yet I didn't, maybe there was a part of me that wanted to test death again, that thought, 'what on earth else can possibly happen to me, what else can I survive?'

I can't really remember the rest of the trip or the flight home. When I had therapy soon after this, the majority of the time my memory focused on the hijacking but the whole thing was horrific. I think for so long my memory was blurred and I didn't have time to process it all, I had to compartmentalise and for a long time I couldn't access all the details. The only thing I remember about that trip is the hijacking, the sharks, the dead man and the car accident and the guy with the gun. The man in the adidas hoody with the gun. Everything else is a blur.

And when I returned to the UK, I didn't have time to process that blur and all that happened because I came back to such chaos in my private life too, and my marriage crumbled soon after that. I was gone in my head at that point. I was done.

But all the papers were interested in were stories about me owing money and being evicted and not paying tax and I remember thinking, if only they knew! And so now, when the papers write stories about me, I think to myself, you won't beat me. You won't get me down again. I am not in the same place I was when I came back from South Africa. I'm a survivor and I won't be broken again.

So there you have it, my hijacking. It's as blunt as that. And although it's horrifying, it's also shown me that a mother's love for her children knows no limit. I was ready to give my life for my children as I sat in the truck in front of them with a cushion over my face, preparing myself to hear the shot from the gun before the bullet entered my body. That never came. I got a second chance at life and I'm not going to waste it.

* * *

I looked back over my notes from the Priory to prepare for this chapter. It was quite intense, seeing everything I had written down, all my thoughts when I was in my darkest place. They gave me printouts of song lyrics and poems and I have pages of them and, as I have mentioned before, if any of the words or the lines of poetry meant anything to you or you felt a connection with them, they encouraged you to underline them. On one page, the poem *Town of Sad* by Anita is typed and I remember being drawn to these lines:

My body and mind, just feels beyond dead.
Right or left, I'm asked to choose.
But I continue along the sidewalk, change I refuse.

I had scribbled some notes next to them, the words are barely readable but I had put: 'This is my chance to prove you can hit rock bottom and make it up the ladder. Never give up.'

The poem, *The Road Not Taken* by Robert Frost, is also in

my notes. I have underlined these lines:

And sorry I could not travel both;

And be one traveller, long I stood.

I doubted if I should ever come back.

I haven't made any notes next to these but I must have felt a connection to them. I remember feeling that I was lost. That perhaps I should have gone down a different path. I am reminded of my sadness when I see them now, but also my strength. Does that make sense?

Some of the therapy sessions are designed to help you focus your thoughts and feelings. They give you sheets of paper that have boxes or diagrams on them with headings and you fill in what you can. There was one form that had on one side, 'Questions to ask yourself', and under-neath the first question was, 'Specifically, what are you predicting will happen?', and my response was 'Scared I'll kill myself.' The box underneath it asks 'How likely (0–100%) is it that this will actually happen?' And I have just written the numbers 99. Then underneath, 100.

The group therapy sessions are varied and designed to help you to exploit an emotion or situation in a safe surrounding. I remember one session they had an empty chair in the middle of the room and they said to me, 'Imagine you could have anyone sitting on that chair, absolutely anyone, and there are things you want to say

One of my first modelling shoots, before surgery. I can't believe I've been doing this for 30 years, but I wouldn't change a thing.

Those early Jordan days were amazing, I can't believe some of the stuff I did. And yes, that's me with Rylan, way back in the day.

Jordan

www.jordanfanclub.co.uk

I'm still so proud that I was the first Brit to ever pose for *Playboy*. Meeting Hugh Hefner and being in the Playboy Mansion was incredible.

The press have vilified me for years – I can't believe some of the stuff they've said about me. © News UK, 2003

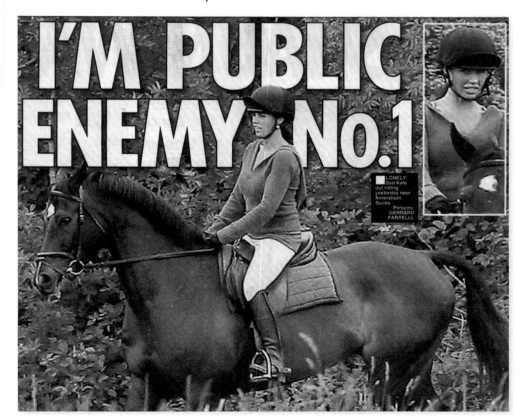

I'm not always done up; I love nothing more than being make-up free in my comfy clothes.

My family, friends
and hobbies mean
everything to me.
They've kept me sane
through it all.

Having Harvey changed my life, and all my babies are the reason I keep on going.

My kids are my world.

to that person. Who would it be and what would you say?'

I chose Kieran. Out of everyone I could have chosen, mine was Kieran and as I imagined him sitting there I began bombarding him with questions. 'Why did you cheat on me? Why did you do all these awful things I'm learning about? Why have you done this to me?' There are lots of other things I asked the chair that I can't repeat here because of legal reasons but let's just say, I was mentally exhausted afterwards. You don't get any answers – obviously! – but I felt so much better afterwards, which I know must sound weird. I think just airing your thoughts and getting things off your chest helps.

I am looking at a worksheet now called 'Vicious Cogs'. There is a large cog in the middle of the page and it's surrounded by smaller cogs around the outside. In the middle cog they ask you to write the name of your problem (I write anxiety, depression, major trauma) and any unhelpful beliefs (I write worry). The smaller cogs around the outside are all the unhelpful things I do to keep the big cog turning. I can barely make out my writing in some of the cogs but I have written words and sentences like 'I don't want to burden people', 'People not wanting me to succeed', 'Confusion', 'Jealousy', 'Failure', 'Exhaustion'. I am sharing all of this because I think talking about these feelings is as real as it gets. I think people often think celebrities or famous people go into the Priory as a bit of a joke, or as a way of getting a bit of time off. I can't answer why other people go there but I needed to work through the trauma of my hijacking, and of Kieran, and of everything else that was causing noise in my head otherwise, as one of my other cogs revealed, I would always live in 'Fear'.

* * *

Art therapy was always interesting. Each session was completely different, you didn't know what they were going to ask you to do. In one session I remembered they told us that we were starting our pictures with a brown door which you could make any size you want and once you've opened that door – whenever you are ready – you have ten minutes to draw whatever is behind that door. Basically, whatever is on your mind that day. I folded my A3 piece of paper and drew a line towards one side and on that smaller side I drew lots of stick figures, all falling or lying down with no names on them. Then on the other side, I drew a big sunshine and a tropical island, and I drew smiling faces on small figures to represent my kids. You don't plan what you are going to draw, you just see what comes out from your mind through the pencil you are holding onto the paper. And more often than not, it's very revealing.

In another art session I remember I drew a picture of

me trying to swim and my head coming to the surface of this imaginary strip of water, and then people above the water holding sticks and bopping me on the head to drown me. It was clear to me afterwards that there was a huge group of people – the media, ex boyfriends – who were trying to keep me underwater.

I think of that arcade game now looking at that drawing, you know the one where you get given a toy hammer and you have to 'bop' down the heads of faces that come up from holes. You earn points if you hit them quickly or hard enough. That's how I felt in those days, I was the one trying to come up for air and as soon as I thought I had made it and was safe, I was hit down again and again and again.

There were lots of good things that came from my time in the Priory and one of those was that you meet people in group therapy from all walks of life and you learn a bit about them. I would listen to other people's stories and some of them would shock me. Not in a 'Fucking hell, you poor sod' type reaction, but more in a 'Is that the reason you are sitting here? Just that?! Fucking hell, you wouldn't last a minute in my life!' I couldn't help but judge. But I know, I know, you can't sit there and think you have it worse, or better, than anyone else, because what affects other people is their business.

Having therapy has taught me valuable lessons. I will

ignore a lot of things now that I would have previously reacted to. I have learnt to accept that things will be said that I have no control over, but that I do have control over my reaction. My strongest reaction now is not to retaliate. Now I say nothing. I ride the tide, I let people say whatever they want. I am a firm believer in fate and that people will eventually destroy themselves if you let them, all I have to do is just stand back and watch.

I was about to put away my Priory notes when a sheet of paper came out, which was the song lyrics to 'Fix You' by Coldplay. I had underlined the words, 'I promise you I will learn from all my mistakes'. Too fucking right.

CHAPTER 9

TRUST

'ONE OF THE WORST FEELINGS IN THE WORLD IS HAVING TO DOUBT SOMETHING YOU THOUGHT WAS UNQUESTIONABLE.'

Unknown

Trust is a funny thing, isn't it? I can count on one hand the people I trust right this minute. That's not because I have spent my years being guarded and hard and dismissive. If you know anything at all about me, you know that's not who I am. I have been let down too many times over the years by people I have trusted and I will not let my guard down so easily again. I have learnt the hard way, so now you have to earn my trust and I don't give it away easily.

When I was writing this chapter, I wondered about what advice I would give to people starting out in this industry.

I think it all boils down to this: how much you trust or how much you are willing to give your trust. That can be a person or a situation. It can be an instinct. It can be what you think is a solid, undeniable fact but if you don't feel that it's right, if you don't 'trust' it, even so-called facts can shatter.

I was a sucker for years when it came to trusting people, an absolute sucker. I always find the good in everyone because I don't like to believe anything else. Which means I have played a part in allowing people to use and abuse me.

Losing trust in people shapes who you are as a person. It's like having a mirror. You have a pristine and beautiful full-length mirror and then one day it falls from the wall. There is now a crack in it. It might be a little chip. or a deeper crack, and while you can still use the mirror, you can still see your reflection, you will always have that crack or chip or dent in it. That won't ever go away. It will have forever spoilt your perfect view. It's not the same. I will never be the same because my trust has been broken too many times.

I know that a lot of people say to me that I open myself up to situations that could potentially cause me upset because I'm too open as a person. People come into my life because they know a lot about me and so I feel that they are on my side. I like to trust those people because they seem to 'get' me and that's the problem. I then get burnt, and I have been burnt in the most horrific of ways. When that happens. . . well, there isn't a lot of hope left, is there?

My mistrust of people has come in waves over the years but it always tends to revolve around men who have used and abused me, and created such a web of lies and fantasy that when I confront them, it seems so completely unimaginable that I end up doubting my own instincts.

I am gutted that there's been so many times when I haven't listened to my gut feelings about something and then I find out later that I was right. It's hard when your emotions are involved, you think they are clouding your judgement. You think to yourself, 'No, this can't possibly be true, I'm overreacting,' but all too often it is.

* * *

Openly talking about my past relationships and all the gory details about Kieran and his cheating in my previous book has helped. It's not just helped me in my under-standing of how a narcissist works (I received a lot of help privately with that in therapy), but it's also helped me realise that I am not alone. I've had countless messages from women who have come forward and told me about their own partners cheating on them and the collective sense of 'What have we done to deserve this?' But that's the problem with men who control the narrative for so long – you can only blame yourself when they cheat. They make themselves out to be so perfect that you think it must be you who is to blame. They make you believe it must be your fault that they're shagging anything with a pair of tits. But it's not! I have learnt so much about trust and setting boundaries from seeing all the times in the past when I have openly trusted men when I've got with them because that's what you do, isn't it? You don't go into a relationship with someone you don't trust, you don't start off that way. I've never had boundaries in any relationship but I do now. Why should a man have passwords to all my accounts? Why should he be able to access my phone at any point? Now I put boundaries in place to protect myself.

The definition of a narcissist and gas-lighter is as follows:

Gaslighter (*noun*): 'A person who uses psychological methods to manipulate someone into questioning their own sanity or powers of reasoning. It's a tactic in which a person, to gain power and control of another individual, plants seeds of uncertainty in another person's mind. The self-doubt and constant questioning slowly cause the individual to question their reality.'

There is a clip from an episode of my show, *My Crazy Life*, way back in 2019 that I would love you to watch. In it, there is an exchange between me and Kieran where I am so angry and so confused and broken. I don't understand why I want to stay with him but I tell him that I love him. And in that exchange, he never once says it back. I remember it all. But now I watch it and I see him for what he really is. He was sat there all smug and smirking, playing the role of helpless, selfless, 'poor me' victim.

Kieran is telling me how I'm perfect for him and all I can see in my face is me thinking, *I am desperate, I can see that but I want him to acknowledge what he has done to me – this is all because of him.* He's asking me how he can heal things, heal the pain he's caused.

His reply is so simplistic, so characteristic of him playing his 'tell me what I can do to make it right because I am so pathetic it's not my fault'.

This was my life for months after the betrayal. I wanted to believe him but he was such a liar and I loved and hated him at the same time.

I'm watching Kieran tell me what he can do to make things better and it reminds me of how much direction he needed, and it just feels like another one of his games.

He's telling me how much he does for everyone, how caring he is and how he wants the change to make it right.

But I didn't just want someone ticking things from a list, I wanted a husband who would be there for me.

Telling me he loves me, it hurts to watch that now after everything we've gone through.

I tell him I love him – not him telling me. He never did, which is quite something when you look back. I'm telling him I shouldn't be with him, I can't forgive him, he shouldn't have cheated on me and yet it's clear that I'm weak and that I'll take him back. He asks me what I would do? Always my responsibility, not his. I can see all the red flags but at the time, I was so in love.

I told Kieran I loved him, again, and again he said nothing.

That's all that needs to be said, really.

* * *

I am always happy to help people. In terms of supporting a charity, or a business, I have helped a lot of people without getting a penny because I know, in this business, a little promotion goes a long way. I never expect something for nothing and I am always happy to pay my own way, so if I am working with a company on a product you best believe that it's something I use and love otherwise I won't put my name to it. If I genuinely like a clothing or beauty brand, I will do social media posts for nothing. I'm not like a normal celebrity who expects something in return.

If I agree to help someone, I will. If I agree to promote a product on social media, I will. But I have found that helping people has its pitfalls and that's the saddest thing. You see, people have worked out that if they say they aren't happy with MY promotion of THEIR product, they can go to the papers with a story about me not helping, or put a post on social media about it, and suddenly they get ten times the amount of publicity – their product is mentioned, my name is mentioned and hey presto, it's some sort of story apparently. I do fewer and fewer of these promotions now as I have had it thrown back in my face too many times. Which is really sad as I naturally want to help people. I don't have a side to me that says, 'what's in it for me?', but I am not sure people see that, or want to believe it. It's just another thing that they have made their minds up about me – that I'm only interested in freebies, money or designer clothes. I would love you to see me now as I'm writing this chapter in a hoody and jodhpurs because I've been out for a hack this morning. It's so glamorous! I never seem to get invited to events now either, yet everyone knows if I turn up, there is a good chance that my photo will get taken and I'll be in the paper and the evening is mentioned and known about. It does make me wonder when people tell me that so-and-so are going to this event or that. . . to me, these people are nobodies! I have achieved more than most of these five-minute, fame-hungry arseholes probably ever will!

If you think about it, I am not sure why I fit into the celebrity category anymore. I am a businesswoman who has brought out a ton of products over the years and I am proud of every single one of them. If I were to list them all now it would take far too long but there have been autobiographies, fiction books, perfumes, clothing lines, underwear, accessories, calendars, albums, children's clothes, equestrian wear, equestrian equipment. . . I could go on. But business success like that doesn't make headlines, does it?

There are a few other people who've come into my life over the years, who I have found it very hard to trust. I have been chased by nine men with cameras down an alleyway and into a car park. I have been hounded as I walk down the streets and they've printed the photos of me looking 'nuts'. But when I have rung the police about the situation, as soon as I tell them my name, they tell me there isn't anything they can do because I'm in the public eye. It's like they are saying, 'Sorry, love, you've brought this on yourself'. But if I was 'Kate Brown' or 'Katie Smith', I'm sure I'd get help. Why am I any different? The feelings that go through my body in that situation – the fear, the adrenaline, the panic – are the same as anyone else would experience, therefore why can't I get the help that anyone else would get?

Chat show hosts took the piss out of me for years.

Graham Norton, Alan Carr. . . they would dress up as me after I'd been on, mocking me or my outfits or my hair. No one called them out on it. It was like I was a character to be made fun of without consequence. What sort of damage does that do to my mental health? When magazines were mocking Britney Spears when she shaved her head and hit out at paps with a brolly, when they recreated that look with other celebrities dressing as her across their pages, how responsible is that? What message does that send out? That anyone struggling with their mental health is fair game?!

Unfortunately, when the chat show hosts took the piss out of my look, getting out the fake tits and big hair, they were taking the piss out of a person, not a character. I am the same person, whether that's Jordan or Kate, I'm not like Lily Savage and Paul O'Grady or Dame Edna and Barry Humphries. I started in the media as Jordan, I never changed my name to Katie Price. I didn't suddenly wake up one day and go, today I'm going to be Katie Price and not Jordan anymore. I am the same person. But no one seemed to understand that.

I just don't trust professionals. Police have let me down, social workers have let me down, managers have let me down and the media have let me down. But I still have hope. I have hope that no matter what happens, or how bad something seems, one day things will get better.

It might be the stubbornness in me but hope keeps me going because I know I am doing all the right things and I won't give up.

And that's why I've got to be positive and focus on the future. I can't tell you how easy it would be for me to tell everyone to, 'Fuck off!' To say to every single person who is on my case in one form or another, 'Fuck off!' But I don't and I won't. I trust that the social workers that come into my home will judge me fairly, I trust that the people who judge me in court do so fairly.

And however much I have been hurt in the past, I would like to build friendships with women again. I have hope that it will happen. I met a couple of people at the gym the other day, girls I hung out with at school. I didn't recognise one of them at first, but she saw me and we got chatting. We have arranged to meet up again and I can't wait. I was friends with them both over 30 years ago so they aren't after a slice of anything, they want to meet me for the girl they knew at school. I am so excited about catching up with them. I can't offer them a showbiz lifestyle, or tickets to events, so I know they just want to meet me for me. For friendship.

When you don't have many friends because they have used you, or broken your trust, it doesn't mean you stop wanting to have mates. I just need to choose more wisely. But I'm a Gemini. I am impulsive and I have an addictive personality and I will continue to trust people. The only thing I feel I am doing wrong in my life at the moment is vape. I know, it's not a very rock and roll life! I have always stayed away from paths that others in the industry went down and avoided people that would have dragged me down and got in the way of my career. My work was, and still is, so important to me. Back in the day if I knew I had a photoshoot to get up for, that was far more important than staying out at a club, partying.

It's the same now. I don't have alcohol in my house and I'm in bed by 8.30 p.m. most nights. I like cups of tea more than anything else. I will occasionally have a glass of Prosecco when I go to the hairdresser's because having a glass with the girls is part of the pamper – everyone gets a glass when they go in. That said, I am a little nervous to do it now. I panic that people will see me having a drink and accuse me of being drunk. I am 46 fucking years old and I am too scared to enjoy a glass of Prosecco because of what it looks like.

It's a joke but not a joke, because this is my life! The worst thing is, I am being told so often that I am this addict, or alcoholic, and it makes me start to question myself. . . am I going nuts? Am I missing something? Am I doing something that everyone else is seeing but I can't? I've asked Lynn our nanny so many times if I am doing something wrong and it's only me that's not seeing it because I really think I must be missing something.

I have whiteboards up around the house of all the kids' activities and my work so they can see and know what's going on. I am sure there are toys and games for the kids to play with and pictures they have drawn all round the house. I am sure there are clean clothes in their wardrobes and food in the fridge and cuddly toys on their beds and me here when they leave and get back from school so what am I missing? What am I not seeing?

I'm damned if I do and I'm damned if I don't. I'm not living any sort of life because I am just so 'on edge' about every decision I have to make. Do I have to be Mary Poppins? I don't know what I have to do. I am sure lots of people are very abusive to social workers who visit them, but not me. Come when you want is all I have ever said.

Again, I have nothing to hide.

CHAPTER 10

DEAR PRESS...

> **'SHE'S DANGEROUS BECAUSE
> SHE KNOWS WHAT IT'S LIKE
> TO FALL AND GET BACK UP
> A THOUSAND TIMES. ROCK
> BOTTOM KNOWS HER NAME
> AND THE ONLY PERSON WHO
> SAVED HER IS HER. SHE IS NOT
> AFRAID OF BREAKING.'**
>
> *S. Bennett-Henry*

We all know I can talk a lot so it shouldn't surprise you to learn that this open letter to the press is going to be a long one. But there are a lot of things I need to get off my 34H chest and while it is very long, I hope that you can see why I've needed to say it. It's like a release valve has gone off in my head and once I get going, I can't stop.

Ironically, I sat down to write this letter the morning I'd read online that my horse, Wallis, had been taken away from me by the bailiffs. The same horse who is outside in the stables like he has been for the past 15 years since I've had him. Princess has just popped by to see me and asked me what's happened to Wallis as she too read about it and has come to see if I'm OK. I think once I've finished writing this I'm going to go out and post a video on Instagram of me giving Wallis a good rub, which mocks the load-of-shit story in the papers. Who would even take a 21-year-old horse anyway?

Apparently, the bailiffs can actually seize animals, according to my mum, who had a conversation about this the other day. And do you know what's horrific? They would take my beautiful horse and they would put him up for auction to see if they could get good money for him. And if he didn't sell, they would take him to the knacker's yard. How is that even fair? How is that even legal? I would be so fucking livid if that ever happened. What sort of monsters would take an animal and not care about their welfare? But the story is a load of bollocks, as is most of what is printed about me. Wallis is safe and well and mostly likely enjoying his morning hay. But that doesn't make a good headline, does it? And talking of headlines, here goes. . .

Dear Press,

Hi. You might not know me but my name's Kate Price. I say this because I don't believe you know me as a person, a human, a woman, a mother, a sister, an aunt, because for the past 30 years I think you've just seen me as a product. A product that you can use and abuse.

I started my journey with you when I was 17 and I'm now 46 years old and the journey I've had with you has had its ups and downs. More ups for you in terms of papers sold, more downs for me in terms of crap I've had to deal with.

From the moment I stepped out in front of the cameras, the flashing bulbs and the shouts and the jeers from my nights out in Chinawhite or Red Cube, I thought the attention was fun. But when I look back, there were always photos that you chose that were taken while I was blinking or stumbling in my heels. You'd choose those dodgy photos and print them to make out I was drunk or something. But at the time I was so young, and so happy that I was in the paper and that you were giving me attention, that I didn't care. I was happy that you had chosen me to be pictured! But really, that was the beginning of a journey of destruction. If I could have a conversation with my 17-year-old self, I would ask her, are you sure that this is what you want to do? Is this life really what you want?

You know what dodgy deals you made over the years. You know what agreements you made behind my back. You know all the supposed 'unplanned' paparazzi shots were set up and you took money for them behind my back and I was none the wiser.

I'd be surprised to see you turn up somewhere I was going, or meeting someone or just out shopping and suddenly the paps would be there and I wouldn't have a clue where you came from. Only you would know and you would be rubbing your hands with glee. But I would like the attention and I would see myself more and more in the papers, like a seed of fame, and I was blooming.

I know you like to remind me that I wouldn't be where I am without you. You've been telling me this for years, in a way that's tried to manipulate me into being grateful or something. Yes, we've had our fun. I have always been up for a laugh with you. I got how it was, I understood how it worked and we played the game together. We played nicely. What other girl in this country is like me and would give you lots of fun with my press calls? I'd dress as a nun or in lots of different costumes and you would love it and I would love it. I'd always put on a good show for you. I loved that part of my job and I loved doing the interviews too but I haven't done any press calls for ages or interviews for ages because if I do one, it doesn't matter what I say, you twist my words.

It's got to a point where it's not fun anymore.

People don't last long in this industry nowadays, there is no one like me who has survived as long as I have. I have ridden the showbiz monster for three decades and I'm still here. I would have thought you'd had your pound of flesh from me by now, but obviously not.

Does that make me fair game? Does that make me an easy target? Because you've always got away with it, you continue to do so. I have been in the spotlight for so long maybe you have forgotten to think of me as a person with feelings.

Does that make it easier to write crap about me because you think I'm not going to mind? To not get upset? Is it because I've never fought back? Is it because you think, 'Oh, it's just her, she doesn't care.' But I do care. I care very much. But you don't. One week there would be a story about me partying, 'Jordan's out on the town again', and then another week, if I'm with my children, 'Katie Price dressing up her kids'. It all depended on the angle you wanted on any particular day, on any particular week.

Anyone can ring you up and tell you a story and you just write it and it's published and then it's out there as 'the truth' for anyone to read. How is that responsible? How is that allowed?

You have constantly, forcefully and brutally attacked me for years and years. Why? You have swayed the public into believing I am a character, a villain. But you don't live at my home, you don't live my life, yet you constantly criticise. You see me on a red carpet, or posing for a press call or on the street doing my shopping and you turn it into a damaging story. What can one woman be doing wrong by going to the shops and getting food? What can I be doing wrong by posing in a bikini?

You invade my privacy. You suffocate me. Home should be a safe place and yet you fly drones over my house and have paps come to the end of my driveway.

You comment on my animals when you don't know the truth. You write stories from sources but what sources are these? Ketchup? HP Sauce?

Those sources aren't my friends. They aren't even real people, you just make it up. I know if my real friends spoke about me, you'd never write any of their stories because it would be about me being nice, about being a good mum, about being a survivor, about being a single parent who's never taken a penny off a man. About a woman who's raised five wonderful children while having some dreadful men in her life who like to use her name, use her generosity and lifestyle and then turn on her. Where are those stories?

Some people say I should be flattered by all the attention, but it's exhausting. Mentally, exhausting. You've seen me going into the Priory, you've seen me asking for help. You know why I went into the Priory; you know it was for severe trauma rehabilitation and PTSD and yet you keep making out it was for addiction to drugs or alcohol. Complete lies.

For 30 years you have written bad stories. How bad can I be to have so many horrible stories written about me? I'm treated like I'm a bloody criminal! I think a murderer would get an easier ride than me and it's got to the point where I question myself and who I am.

Am I the way I am because I've had to defend myself so often? The way I speak now, about traumatic events that have happened to me in the past, is so matter of fact, so detached from emotion, it's not normal. Yet I've normalised it because that's the only way I can deal with it. But I know that's not right, I know talking like I do about it is not a normal response.

I want to get on with my life, I want to move

on, but you make it very hard. I can't remember, I honestly can't remember, the last story that you wrote about me that was positive. And even if it had been positive, you would turn it into a negative in some way. You can't just leave a full stop and say 'Well done' and that's the end of it.

I've learnt not to Google my name anymore. I used to do it endlessly when I was younger, but I try not to now in an act of self-preservation.

I told my older children never to Google me and, for now, I tell my younger children, they should be proud of me, and if they ever read stories about me that aren't nice it's because some people are against me but they must remember that people only want to write stories about people who have achieved something – if I hadn't, no one would care about me.

There was a particularly awful time when you made a story up about my mum and I will probably never forgive you for it. You had written a story and said she had commented on something, when in actual fact, my mum was in intensive care having a lung transplant. There was absolutely no way she could have commented on anything because she was in a coma. It was impossible! That had a terrible effect on the family as we didn't want to tell the world that Mum was having an operation, that she was seriously ill, but we had to release a statement so people knew what lies you had been spouting.

I've been tarnished for so long by you that no 'big' managers want to work with me because of the reputation I have, which is down to the things they have read and think they know. Everyone has an opinion on me but very few of those opinions are based on meeting me, but instead based more on what stories you have written about me that day. What the public don't know is this industry is full of managers who are in with the papers. Never has the phrase 'it's not what you know but who you know' been more truthful about this industry and this world.

Each workplace has their own world, doesn't it? It's run very effectively and efficiently and there is a hierarchy. You know that perhaps someone might not be as good at their job as you are, but they are the ones that get promoted. Mostly, it's because they are in with the right people. It's the same in my world. You could be the most famous TV presenter in the country, be live on TV every Saturday night, be winning more awards than I've had boob jobs, and yet if you do something wrong, don't worry. If you crash your car because you are well over the drink driving limit, and you cause a child in the car you hit to believe they are 'dying' because they are in so much shock, and you are given the highest fine ever thought to be imposed by a UK court for drink driving, and you are banned from the road for nearly two years, again, don't worry. The story will be swept under the carpet in a matter of days. You've got good people around you, they will promote your mental health and your poor state of mind and you'll be given another chance by the public because of the stories that are spun in your favour. So don't worry.

Oh, the people I saw when I was in the Priory, the famous faces that would be in there for their drug addictions – some of the biggest coke heads you've ever seen, who everybody would recognise – but you'll never read about them because they are protected. If you are with the right crowd and the right management you'll get away with murder. You'll probably even come out with a TV award at the end of it. The media, the press all play this game. They all know it's the case, they especially know that often the people who are being betrayed as whiter than white are the worst – yet they have this protective bubble around them. Their management seem to have the right editors, the right TV executives, the right people in their pocket.

It's so corrupt, and you know it's corrupt. You allow yourself to be dictated to by the management of this little clan, this group of celebrities, the same old faces. They are their own media Mafia.

But when I go to the Priory, it's frowned upon. Others get away with it. Others can play the 'I need help, it's not my fault' card and all is forgiven, yet I have been asking for help for years – and for someone as headstrong and independent as me, it's the hardest thing I've had to do, and I will continue to do so because I know it's the right thing to do. But you still find a way to put me down, to target me when I ask for help.

The refreshing thing is when people do meet me, they tell me how different I am and how shocked they are – but I genuinely get embarrassed meeting new people because I don't know what they have, or haven't, read. I want to get t-shirts printed that say, 'Don't believe everything you read!' or that say, 'Please don't question me about anything, I'm exhausted'.

The hardest thing is, if a story comes out that is particularly brutal, I still have to go about my day. I still have to go to the shops, or pop out to the gym and see my photo on a magazine staring back at me. I want to tell everyone who stops for a look, 'Don't believe any of that!' I have actually done that quite a few times. I've tapped on someone's shoulder as I've seen them reading some crap about me in the newspaper and I have politely said that they shouldn't believe it, that it's all rubbish. They smile and hurriedly shut the paper, looking embarrassed, and then scuttle off. I don't mean to embarrass them, and I don't want them to feel bad, I just want them to understand that what they are reading is untrue or has been twisted. I think I want people to remember there is a real person behind every story you write. It would be funny if it wasn't so serious. It's like my life is an episode of *EastEnders*. It seems like fiction to most people, like all the drama can't possibly be real, but it is and it's my life. Imagine how exhausting that is. It's why I have days when I don't want to show up. I have days when I think, 'No, I'm not going to give any more because I know it will get thrown back in my face.'

I think I would also like to understand more about why you don't recognise all that I have done. I get a lot of 'worst this' or 'worst that' awards – 'worst dressed' being the most often. That's OK, I don't mind. I know if I wear certain things I bring attention to my fashion sense and I know it's not for everyone. I did have a glimmer of hope that, going through some of the ordeals I have suffered, perhaps you would be more sympathetic towards me. Perhaps you would give me some credit for surviving a number of things that many people would struggle to comprehend, let alone live through. I wouldn't wish some of the stuff I have been through on my worst enemies, but instead of being shown a little compassion, you see my head surface from the water and push me back down again. All the time I am trying to get up for air, you are busy drowning me with the weight of the papers you have sold or the magazine stories you write. It's survival for me but it's just sales for you.

In all honesty, what you write about me is irrelevant. Some of the more recent stuff is like a broken record. I know I'm bankrupt, this isn't news to me, but I don't need the countless stories, the endless fabrications about my situation. Every. Fucking. Day. Everyone has money issues and people are facing bankruptcy for all sorts of reasons but why is it constantly me? Saying my horse was taken – it was a total lie! Being fixated on my financial issues is a mystery to me but you know the damage it causes. You seem to like to rub it in my face but for what reason? Why do I have to explain myself to you?

Other countries embrace success. They want to

celebrate talent, or people who are doing well and faces that have been around in the spotlight for years and years, but not here, not me.

Why don't you surprise me and start playing ball and maybe start embracing me as something good that has come out of Britain? Wouldn't that be a turn up for the books? If you did that all the trolls – who seem to think they know me because of what you have written – will stop being so rude, aggressive and vile. I get so much hatred online that it sometimes feels you are actively trying to destroy me. I'm not being dramatic, or causing a fuss over nothing, or making a mountain out of a mole hill. It feels like I'm – very openly and brazenly – being attacked for the sole purpose of breaking me. The online world is a sinister place to be. I hope you choose your targets carefully because I know many people that won't survive there. We all know the victims of your hounding.

Social media links and stories are the worst. The comments are unrepeatable. Back when I started in this fame game, at least a story that was printed in the paper was discarded the next day. Fish and chip shop paper after 24 hours, that's what they said. But not anymore.

I remember several times in the past I had your

paps trying to take me to court because I had accidentally run over their feet. Seriously! I mean, follow me and chase me down the road and launch yourself at my car to get a photo of me or my children but oh, the uproar if you get a bit too close and forget I'm driving a heavy car and am not worried about twinkle-toed paps. Have you ever tried driving while being blinded by a million camera flashes going off? It's quite a skill I've honed over the years. Or trying to get into a vehicle and then out of a car parking space while you've been on my bonnet and at my window and running across the road. I wonder if this should be part of a driving test scenario for the new generation of wannabe celebs. And woe betide me if I have a male passenger in the car, then the chase is on! Then I know we definitely won't be left alone because this is a whole new angle, a whole new story and a whole new wad of cash to line your pocket if the pap gets the right shot.

It's very hard to start relationships – you understand, right? If I go for dinner with a male friend, I'm suddenly dating them. How am I meant to do anything normal? I am a normal girl, I try and do normal things but everything is different for me. I have to look out for a camera phone round every corner. I am never rude to people when I am out and about but trying to have a meal in peace with everyone trying to sneak a photo is hard. Then that someone sells a photo of you and then my phone goes mental because I am being messaged with a million questions. 'Are you seeing JJ, Kate?' But maybe I don't want to say anything just yet. I don't want to confirm or deny it. Maybe we need time to announce our relationship without you calling the shots. I have ruined relationships before they've started because they have to be brought into this fucking world. My world. Of course I warned JJ. Having been on *Married at First Sight*, he was sort of aware of it all. But it's hard when you are meeting people for the first time. I'll sometimes try and make a joke of it. I'll try and call out the elephant in the room straight away and say, 'By the way, I'm not like this and I'm not like that.' I don't want people, especially men who I want to start a relationship with, to come with preconceived ideas about me, which are often a load of crap. Which is why JJ and I spent time getting to know each other before we went public, before we wanted intrusion and the hounding that was bound to come.

Which brings me to the reason for this letter. After 30 years in this industry, I want to make a deal with you. Stop. Stop with the bullying. I don't care if you never write anything about me again.

I genuinely don't. But you won't. You'll write whatever the hell you want as you always do. People don't understand why I don't just walk away, why some people say to me, 'If you don't like what they're doing, just quit', but it's all I know. I love doing TV shows, and if I was bad at it, how have I survived for so long?

I want you to know you can't beat me. So the joke's on you, isn't it?

I want you to know I wake up every day with a fire in my belly and no matter what lies you write about me, what made-up stories or hurtful features you produce, you won't be able to extinguish that. I love every aspect of what I do and I still have that excitement and that drive to work. You can't, and you won't, ever take that away from me and I will continue to rise despite all that you do. I won't rise from the ashes, I'm the whole fucking fire and it will take more than what you are ever capable of to bring me down again.

Kate

CHAPTER 11

BODY DYSMORPHIA

'HAVE I EVER FELT HAPPY WITH HOW I LOOK? SIMPLE ANSWER: NO.'

About five minutes before I started writing this chapter, I emailed my surgeon. I know I said earlier that I didn't, but I have decided I want smaller boobs. So I will, it's as simple as that! I have been called butch, hench and stocky online recently and although I don't take notice of trolls, I had a real look at myself and I do look a lot heavier with bigger boobs.

I like to wear tracksuits, comfy stuff like hoodys and oversized jumpers, but they can make you look bigger than you are, even if you don't have particularly big boobs. But I do, and clothes end up hanging over them and it's hard to see anything below. It depends what I feel I look like at the time. When I did *Big Brother*, I had to have them taken out the day after leaving the house because they had become really infected. They were out for about three or four months, which meant I could wear clothes that I hadn't worn for years. Different clothes to my normal style. I could wear shirts that were more open and subtle. It was probably classed as more fashionable. I looked smaller and for a while I quite liked it. But I prefer having bigger boobs. I couldn't work out, if I tried, how many boob jobs I've had. It's definitely not as many as Google makes out though. Well, I don't think so anyway.

Yes, I've decided. I want to go smaller. I've got back into my horse riding again and I'm going to the gym on a regular basis. I want to have more of an athletic, smaller body. I want my small body back. But I still want to look like I have big boobs, just not this big anymore.

It's really hard to answer the question about exactly what bra size I am because I only know what the size of my implants are – 2500cc! I did go to Marks & Spencer, Ann Summers, Bow and Victoria's Secret to be measured and they all came up with a completely different size. I couldn't even buy any bras in Victoria's Secret or Bow, the only place I could was Ann Summers and they measured me to be a 34H so that's what we'll go with. I am looking at boobs now; I want to get myself booked in soon, the idea has got me all excited. I will look thinner if I'm a bit smaller. Perhaps I will start wearing a bra if I go smaller too. I don't wear them as a rule as I find them very uncomfortable. I would wear them for photoshoots or a specific event if required but they dig into my back. I don't even like wearing knickers, I don't like anything on. I don't slug in my pants, I slug in my trousers. That's the only difference. The only time I wear knickers is if I am wearing a skirt and I haven't worn a skirt for ages. When was the last time you saw me in one? Or a dress? I never wear them because I can never find any that fit me nicely. I suppose that's because they have to be a certain size across my chest, which means they swamp the rest of me. Can you imagine me wearing a floaty, floral number? It wouldn't suit me and it would look terrible! The only dresses that do fit me have to be Lycra based and then I fall into the trap of looking like a Russian hooker.

I've just texted my mum and told her about the surgery. She won't be happy with that. I haven't finished with surgery, I know that much so I need to tell her it will either be now or in a few months but I will be having something done. Who knows, in years to come maybe I will get to a point when I say to myself, 'I'm happy now', but I'm not there yet. My mum thinks I have body dysmorphia and a few other people say the same. The only thing I know is that if you can change something you don't like, then why not do it? If you have a headache, do you leave it? Ignore it? Put up with the pain? No, of course you don't. Well, I know I don't. You take a tablet and you change it.

If you have a big hairy mole on your face and you don't like it, why not remove it? That's all cosmetic surgery really is, changing something because you don't like it.

But as I've got older, I realise this stems from deeper issues. I never thought I was pretty, even when I was younger. I still don't think I'm pretty. That's why I have surgery. I could have a million people tell me I'm pretty but I won't believe any of them. That's just who I am. I can scrub up alright, I suppose, if I have to. But I want to look like a Bratz doll now, that's my aim. There is a surgeon I see on Instagram and he makes all the girls look the same and I'm like, 'I want it!' I say to whoever is with me, 'I want to look like that!' They think I'm crazy but I love it.

Everyone's perception on what looks beautiful is different, isn't it? I have been told countless times over the years to stop with the surgery because men prefer the natural look, but fuck that. I just love changing my look, maybe that's my creative side coming out.

I have never, ever had any surgery done to get more work or for a work commitment. I always knew I wanted my boobs done. *The Sun* ran a poll on me when I first started doing Page 3, asking people to vote about whether I should or not, and there was a high percentage of readers that said for me not to do it. But me being me, of course I did. I wanted them done, so I did. All my surgery is done for me, no one else. I have had lots of people try and stop me over the years, but no one can talk me out of it when I make my mind up. I would never advise anyone to have any kind of surgery though. Not to boost their career, in modelling or acting or showbiz or whatever.

I remember always wanting big boobs from a young age, I always put so many pads in my bra. I was frigid at school but if boys touched my boobs, they would know there was more padding than anything else!

The whole process of going under anaesthetic is fun for me. I love trying to fight back against the urge to fall asleep and then when I wake up, I have something new. It helps with my needle anxiety too. I never worry that I won't wake up or that something will go wrong. It's never bothered me at all because I am doing something that I want to do. I get excited about it. Is that a strange thing to say?

The only time I get nervous is when I have surgery that I haven't chosen to do. Having the operation on my feet, for example, I was absolutely petrified. It was a totally different mindset. All I could think was, 'Something is going to go wrong.' My brain was in overdrive. When it's something I want, it's fine – I suppose because it's within my control. I got no sympathy when I had that operation on my feet. I think for some reason people thought I was faking it! No one showed any compassion even though I had life-changing injuries and was in a wheelchair with two casts on my feet – people still thought it was a publicity stunt. I mean, really?! I have 14 screws in my feet, I didn't want to break them! I screamed with the pain when it happened. It was horrific. We were in Turkey because I was having my teeth done and I was messing around with Junior and Princess outside the front of the hotel. It was in the evening and I was pretending I was a galloping horse and jumping around when I jumped over this bush and fell down a 20ft drop onto a concrete car park. I tried to get up and I couldn't. It felt like I had no feet. Oh my God, that pain was worse than giving birth to Harv.

I got taken to hospital and they told me I had a hairline fracture. They wanted to operate on me straight away but I didn't have any holiday insurance so they put a cast on me and when I got back to the UK I went to see a private foot doctor to be assessed because in my mind, a hairline fracture shouldn't be as painful as it was. I was in agony! Even Junior was like, 'Come on, Mum!' as in, why was I making such a fuss? The doctor took my cast off and my feet were black underneath and this hideous shape. They were shocked; they said it was a similar injury to what someone who commits suicide would have when they jump from buildings, or Paras in the army who land wrongly. 'Kate, who told you it was just a hairline fracture?' said the doctor. 'I don't know if you are going to walk again. You have smashed your feet.' I had to learn to walk again after my operation and they are still not right. I am going to run again though. I want to do a marathon again as I don't want to be told I can't do something. Thats me all over, isn't it? I won't be told. I have started training on the treadmill at the gym. I have to take things so slowly but I will do it. Even if I have to do it in my Airboots, I will do it. JJ will love that, he loves my Airboots. Ha!

Maybe I don't want to go smaller with my boobs now. I'm scrolling through Instagram and I can see girls with big boobs. Do I change mine? Perhaps I shouldn't go smaller. . . Should I go bigger? The girl I am looking at has a tiny waist. Are my boobs bigger than hers? I can't work it out. Some girls look hideous after their surgery. I see some and think, 'I never want to look like that.' I am staring at a girl now who is rough. . . she's had more surgery than hot dinners. That's a full-time job looking like she does with all her make-up on, fuck that. It's awful. She obviously wants people to think she looks like a doll and is pretty but I think she looks fucking awful. Not that she will care what I think, I am sure. The same way that I don't care what other people think about my surgery.

I like the big tits look but I don't dress to show my tits off. This is what people find confusing about me. Why do I have surgery to get bigger boobs when I don't go out in skimpy tops and show them off? I never show them off unless I'm doing OnlyFans now. I love doing that. I do it for myself. When girls, like the ones I am seeing on Instagram, have their boobs done, it's because they want to flaunt them in next-to-nothing tops and to post hundreds of photos of themselves on social media. You'll never see me doing that. If I dress up, I do it for myself, I don't do it for anyone else. I might put up one photo but never the hundreds some girls do. It's usually the younger generation who do it. They need that constant exposure. I think they feel some sort of validation from the number of followers or likes they have. It's different starting out in the business now. They need to know how many people are looking at them, what comments they get. When I did Page 3, I didn't have a clue how many papers were sold and what it all meant, I just got paid to do it. Back then, I loved dressing in the American old-school *Playboy* look. When I was much younger I'd go out with little skirts on but that's what all the girls did in those days and I wouldn't go out dressed like it now, it would look mutton! I don't want to go and show my deck off. I know what I've got, I don't need to flaunt it.

Do I worry about getting old? I'm 46, I wouldn't say I was that old! I just love changing how I look, but I don't want to be a surgery role model for anyone.

I don't want anyone copying me because if they do, they are doing it for the wrong reasons. The only reason you should have surgery is because you want to. I am sure I will talk to Princess and Bunny at some point in their lives about it, but I've probably put them both off for life. The younger generation are on a different path and I'm not sure I can keep up.

Mum's texted back. 'You need to be calm before you do anything, this is something you do because there is a big drama. Your body has enough stress without this.' I'll have to reply to her. She seems to think whenever I have a trauma or stress in my life or when things are out of control, I have surgery. But it's not that, it's all the time with me. I just like having a change. If I want to go blonde, (although I like being dark), I get a wig. It's the same for other people – they have hair or eyelash extensions, or permanent make-up, or eyebrow tattoos. I don't think it's a big deal. 'Mum, it's fine, don't worry,' is all I voice note her back. I imagine she'll roll her eyes when she gets it.

I just like change sometimes. I do want to go smaller, I am obsessed with the gym now, I want to look thinner. I want my bones to stick out just by my hips. . . I know what I want to look I like.

Besides, I heal really well after surgery; it's not traumatic for me. I think I would be really good at giving people advice before they have surgery. Telling them the things that I have learnt. I would tell them not to just look at the 'before' and 'after' photos of people, because those photos can be filtered. Try and meet the person if you can so you can see for yourself what they look like. I never hide away after I have surgery, you never see a before photo of me and then a month later, see me and I'm looking different. I always post the 'in-between' photos or I will be out and about with bandages across my nose with a swollen face.

I don't even worry when I first see myself after surgery, especially if it's on my face and I see all the swelling. I do look beaten up but I am used to that now and I don't mind that look. My kids are used to it too.

You can't ever accuse me of not being completely honest about how it can look when you have surgery because I share the hideous photos so that people can see the reality. I'm not ashamed. It's bloody painful afterwards and you do have to wait a while to heal, but, touch wood, I've never had a bad experience. Yes, of course, I've heard horror stories – especially about surgery abroad – but in my experience, it's far better than in the UK. It's very expensive here and I don't think they are as up to date. I've had it done in America, Belgium and Turkey so I do know what I'm saying. I wouldn't have surgery in America ever again because I really didn't like the after-care. Turkey is cheaper but do your research. I have been told to try Thailand for my face, so I might go there, but I do like Turkey. I am confident that they won't fuck up my face otherwise it will make them look bad because they will get a lot of publicity from me so it's in their interests to do their job well! I've just had a text from a new surgeon I might see, his secretary has said he hasn't had any deaths. That's good to know! Ha!

Have I ever felt happy with how I look? No, never. I did my own make-up on my wedding days, I didn't have time to get the professional treatment so even then I don't think I felt I looked good. I suppose I feel OK when I've had a photoshoot and I've been airbrushed in the photos. I love a filter now so I use them all the time too. I can't help the way I am. I know I'm in the public eye and that there are girls who want to look like me, but I find it bizarre because *I* don't want to look like me. I want to look like other girls. You might look at me and think I look pretty or maybe 'OK', but I never see that myself. I suppose it's the same with how we all go for different types of people, we all know what looks good to us and it's the same within ourselves. What I think looks good, to other people looks rank. I am sorry but I can't explain it any better than that. I can't wait to have surgery again now, it's on my mind.

How would I describe myself? In my head, I am still doing the same thing I did in the Jordan days, because I do the OnlyFans page. When I was Jordan, it was *FHM* or *Playboy* or Page 3, now it's for people who pay on a website. I have adapted and grown with the times. I have absolutely no idea what the younger generation know me for, they wouldn't have a clue who Jordan is. I am just Katie Price on TikTok. Or Princess's or Harvey's mum. I post some photos of me back in the day and it's so weird because I get people asking, 'Is this really you?' Yes, it's really me and yes, I've been around this long! Youngsters these days wouldn't last five minutes! I was having a clear-out in my dressing room yesterday and I found a couple of awards I had won, a Woman of the Year Award from *Cosmopolitan* and Sexiest Girl of the Decade for Jordan. Or something like that. People these days have no idea.

CHAPTER 12

ADHD

'ATTENTION DEFICIT HYPERACTIVITY DISORDER IS CHARACTERISED BY A PERSISTENT PATTERN (AT LEAST SIX MONTHS) OF INATTENTION AND/OR HYPERACTIVITY – IMPULSIVITY THAT HAS A DIRECT NEGATIVE IMPACT ON ACADEMIC, OCCUPATIONAL, OR SOCIAL FUNCTIONING.'

Questions in Childhood:

Difficulty following instructions? Tick.

Starts tasks but quickly loses focus and is easily sidetracked? Tick.

Not completing things? Tick.

Not completing homework or handing it in? Tick.

Questions in Adulthood:

Does things that are muddled up and doesn't complete them. Tick.

Starts tasks but quickly loses focus and is easily sidetracked? Tick

Needs a time limit to complete tasks? Tick.

I hate labels. I don't think they serve a purpose. But a diagnosis? That's different. Being diagnosed with severe ADHD has helped me understand why I am like I am. It's helped me understand why I have behaved in ways I have. It felt like a positive step forward because it was as if someone had looked inside my brain and said, 'This is why you find things hard, Kate. Your brain is wired differently.' It felt like a validation for all the things that I was experiencing. I had all the most common signs – difficulty focusing, problems listening, overspending, forgetfulness, indecision – and on 31 October 2022, I was diagnosed with ADHD combined presentation type 314.01. In the box that indicated whether my diagnosis was mild, moderate or severe, severe is ticked. The diagnosis came about to keep my mum and family happy. 'Kate, you're not right, why do you do this? Why do you do that?' These were things they were constantly saying to me. Or 'Kate, why are you so impulsive? Why do you react like this?' That's what I got all the time from Mum, so in the end I was like, 'OK, I'll go and see the doctor then.'

I wanted to share with you my notes from my doctor who diagnosed me. He rang me while I was having a tattoo done in Thailand and he asked me what I thought his diagnosis might be.

'I don't know, I think I'm nuts!' was my reply. 'My head just doesn't stop!'

Have a read and then I'll continue.

March 24th, 2023

Dear Dr XXXX

Katie was assessed on October 31st, 2022, and followed up on November 24th, 2022, March 6th, 2023, and March 24th, 2023. This followed an indirect referral from a psychologist for an assessment to determine whether Katie might have symptoms consistent with ADHD. The assessment was spread over a larger number of sessions than usual due to issues with Katie's calendar and her intermittently arriving late.

She attended the first session with her step-father Paul, who she referred to as 'Dad', and he corroborated the information provided by Katie. Her mother also completed rating scales for ADHD symptoms, which are appended.

PRESENTING COMPLAINTS

On asking Katie about her primary difficulties at present she reported the following:

1. 'Some of my reactions to things have caused trouble. I've had to learn how to not react. Things build up and then there is an explosion'.
2. 'I would like to not say yes to anything. . . I'm a people-pleaser'.

FAMILY HISTORY

Parents divorced when she was three years old.

Mother remarried her stepfather (Paul – calls him Dad). He works in fencing and building work. She has a maternal half-sister through this relationship.
She has two paternal half-sisters. One of them is being assessed for ADHD.

PERSONAL HISTORY

Born	Brighton
Milestones	Normal
EDUCATION	
	Davidor Infant School
Primary School (5–11 years old)	*Summer Hill Primary, Hove (5–6 years old)* Molested in the park and remembers little else. *Patcham Junior, Patcham (6–11 years old)* They said I was a dreamer.
Secondary School (11–16 years old)	*Patcham Senior, Patcham (11–13)* Problems with focus and concentration. *Blatchington Hill (13–16)* Problems with focus and concentration.
WORK	
17–present	Modelling (The Sun) Film Crews *(NB, I did not go into the details of Katie's career in further details, but understand that this has been somewhat chaotic and that she is a public figure.)*
HOBBIES	(7–present): Horses / riding – this has been a longstanding passion.

DRUG AND ALCOHOL HISTORY

Nicotine	Nil
Alcohol	Rare
Cocaine	2017: started using cocaine **Made her completely quiet.** 2020: Using regularly – allowed her to block everything out.

RELATIONSHIP HISTORY

'Main problem in my life has been men'.

Name	Years	Information
		NB: The details of Katie's relationship history were complicated and I did not explore all the details. I understand that some of them have been public figures. Katie was happy to discuss them further, but this did not seem necessary for the purposes of my assessment.

MEDICAL HISTORY

Medical	'Hole in heart and healed'. Katie reported the absence of significant cardiac issues.
Operations	Cosmetic surgery Fractured feet in Turkey – jumped 20 feet – screws in both feet. Wheelchair for 10 months. Had to learn to walk again. C-section
Medicine:	Escitalopram 5mg

PSYCHIATRIC HISTORY

Year	
7	Molestation
18	**Overdose** (After partner, Gary, cheated on her)
28	Via GP – suggested escitalopram – has been on and off since.
34	Went back on escitalopram (relationship issues) Weaned off to 2.5mg and trying to get pregnant

36	Went back on escitalopram + diazepam (relationship issues) +(therapist)
40	**Attempted to hang self with microphone wire in toilet**
40	Admitted to Priory – after being held at gunpoint and raped in front of children. Diagnosed with PTSD Priory: 6 weeks Treatment: Escitalopram Therapy: Group + EMDR
43	Treatment: Escitalopram Therapy: (1:1) and Group therapy

MENTAL STATE EXAMINATION

Appearance	Casual dress, normal grooming and hygiene
Behaviour	Open and unguarded
Eye contact:	Good
Speech	Fluency or Flow of Speech: Normal rate. Slightly faster than usual Volume: Loud Prosody or Intonation: Normal

Mood	Normal (euthymic)
Affect	Stable
Enjoyment	Fine
Energy	Fine
Sleep	Fine
Appetite	Fine
Concentration	Poor
Thought Process	Linear
Thought Content	Suicidal ideation: Nil
Perceptions	No hallucinations or delusions during interview
Orientation	Oriented to time, place, situation
Insight/ Judgement	Good

OPINION

ADHD Combined presentation type (DSM-V 314.01)

* * *

In the same way that I wanted to find out as much as a I could about PTSD and how that affects other people, I also started looking into ADHD and I found that more and more women my age are being diagnosed with it. Sharing my notes is important both in that it might help you under-stand my life to that point and may help to explain how women my age get diagnosed later in life. My mum was right after all. She and my dad had to fill out all these forms about what I was like as a child, how I reacted to things, what I was like in school and my behaviour. I could remember some bits of my childhood – how I thought I coped with school work and authority, but of course your parents see and remember things differently than you. Looking at my behaviour between the ages of five and 12, my mum answered 'very often' to things like 'Talked excessively', 'lost things necessary for a task or activity', 'blurted out answers before questions had been completed', 'easily distracted' and 'forgetful'. For others like 'fidgeted with their hands or squirmed in their seats', 'left their seats when sitting was expected' and 'appeared restless', Mum all scored as 'often'. Although I always thought I was a little bit different as a youngster – your parents see things much clearer.

But Mum could see it in me as an adult too and those traits are harder to spot because we mask or hide our emotions and feelings and anxieties so well. Mum answered how some of the problems she had marked down as me displaying 'very often' as a child were still interfering with my life in the past six months and it was like someone holding a mirror up, seeing it written in black and white: 'To what extent do the problems you have circled on the previous page interfere with her ability to function in each of these areas of life activities?' Mum had circled areas such as: 'home life', 'immediate family', 'dating or marital relationships', 'management of money', 'driving of a motor vehicle' and 'management of her daily activities'.

I knew I hated asking for help and I would put my irritability or lack of concentration down to hormones or being tired. I know other women who do the same. That we can't articulate how we are feeling because we don't like admitting we can't cope or that we are struggling. Then we feel ashamed. Being diagnosed helped me to understand some of my behaviour. Two things in particular stood out to me about my condition:

'Chronically stressed, potential outcomes for undiagnosed women mean they may depend on prescription medications to manage anxiety, mood disorders, sleep or pain, they may medicate with alcohol or drugs.' That's just me, isn't it?

'By adulthood, women with ADHD may present with substance abuse or compulsive shopping or gambling. They may describe sensory overload, with hypersensitivity to touch, sound, light, or smells. They are more likely to have experienced early physical or sexual abuse and may manifest symptoms related to PTSD.' Again, it's like someone is describing me.

People sometimes say to me, 'Fucking hell, Kate, I don't know how you're not a crumbling mess', and I think to myself, I was. I was a crumbling mess. But I have come through the other side and I have learnt that whatever trauma you have had in life, there is no point sitting and crying about it. You have to help yourself because no one else will. I know that whatever trauma I have been through, I have come out the other side. I have learnt to help myself too. I am doing a course on Dialectical Behaviour Therapy (DBT). I am doing it so that I can help understand what happened to me in South Africa and learn how better to deal with it. The main ideas are to help you to live in the moment, to develop ways to cope with stressful situations or triggers and to help regulate your emotions. I think it was originally for certain mental health conditions but it's a way of helping you regulate your emotions and used for people like me who have suffered post-traumatic stress disorder.

I am strong and I have learnt about how to react to things differently now. Of course, there is never a day that goes by when there isn't drama in my life, but I can't control that. What I can control is how I respond to it.

For example, on Instagram, I don't take pops at people because it doesn't get me anywhere and it just makes headlines, which then make the situation a whole lot worse. So instead, if I find myself wanting to react, I just air it to people around me. Pretty much every time they say to me, 'Kate don't do it'. So I don't. In the past I would not have listened to them, I would have thought that I knew better and would have charged in with a comment in an act of defiance. That's what I did, I was constantly being 'reactive'. I didn't know how to control my head. Knowing what I know now, I would have understood why I needed to send these messages, why I had a 'need' to react.

Since being diagnosed with ADHD, it has helped other people understand me more too – especially my mum. Mum is all about medication but I don't believe it is the solution to everything. I know that going to the therapist helps me and I now know how to quieten myself when I'm in a situation that I might find overwhelming. I will say to myself, 'Calm Kate, calm Kate,' which is just one of my techniques that help. I had so many years of struggling with paperwork in the past. I really struggled to concentrate to fill out one of the simplest forms. I would put things off and so all the letters and paperwork that people were constantly asking me for piled up because my brain couldn't process everything that was being asked of me. You might get a form to fill in and sit down and do it without a problem, but for me it requires tremendous concentration and I very quickly become distracted by anything and everything else because it's so hard. I don't ask for help either so I just ignore it and hope it goes away and of course it doesn't.

I take 20mg of Escitalopram once a day for anxiety, something that I have been taking on and off since I was 28 years old. I was also given ADHD meds when I was diagnosed but I didn't think they worked for me. They wanted me to take medication called Elvanse but I spoke to the doctor about changing them. My mind is so active and I sometimes find it very hard to sleep so I will take sleeping pills when situations are happening in my life that make my brain 'flabbergasted'. Sleep is so important to me and I can't cope if I can't sleep. I am so scared of that ever happening again. I haven't taken any medication for my ADHD for about three months now, there's also been a shortage and I can't get hold of any – but I am OK, I've survived this long and I have also learnt to control myself too.

My brain feeling 'flabbergasted' isn't a new thing. The recent court cases I have been dealing with, for example, all my stuff with the bailiffs, the press, the bankruptcy people. . . my brain is constantly asking the question, 'What the fuck is going on?' Sometimes I get answers to that question and sometimes I don't. I used to be the queen of saying, 'I'm fine, I'm fine, I'm fine'. I still probably do it but to a lesser extent now, but it used to be an instant reaction to anything that was wrong. I would hold or rub my head and all the time I was displaying characteristics of ADHD. I couldn't process a lot of stuff and I had more than my fair share to process.

There have been times in the past when I feel like I am being dictated to in every area of my life. I am trying desperately to control what is going on but I sometimes feel that I am just a piece of meat being thrown around, being controlled by everyone else. Hence why it's so important for me to see my therapist regularly. Then I feel like I'm in a good place.

Now I am in a good place, it's like I have a reset button that I have pressed and I am back in control again.

CHAPTER 13

MY FOUR-LEGGED FRIENDS

> **'HORSES SEE THE REAL YOU.**
> **BEING SEEN IS INCREDIBLY**
> **HEALING.'**
> *Meg Kirby, Founder of The Equine*
> *Psychotherapy Institute*

It's sad that I have to write a chapter about animals but I think a lot of people think I am some sort of pet killer and I want you all to know the truth and not just the shit that the press have made up. Because when stories come out about me not looking after my animals it makes me SO angry because they have been, and will always be, a constant in my life. If you think I am someone who gets rid of my animals, or who kills them, please consider this chapter as hearing the truth about all those vile and horrible stories, straight from the horse's mouth.

* * *

'Have you been using my cheque book?' Mum was so mad at me. 'Katrina! Did you try and write a cheque for that rabbit?' She was absolutely fuming and I couldn't deny it either because I had. I had stolen her cheque book and I had sent the pet shop a forged cheque but only because she didn't buy me the rabbit when I asked!

I was seven years old and we were living at 42 Solway Avenue in Patcham. I can remember it clear as day because I had a gerbil when I lived there and when it died, I buried it in the back garden. But for ages afterwards I would dig it back up again because I hated the idea that he had died and was alone in the ground.

Just up the road from my nan's house was a place called Peter's Pet Shop in Woodingdean in Brighton. I went in there with my mum when we'd been round to see Nan and I remember they had a black rabbit for sale. I really wanted this rabbit, it was £5 and I begged and begged my mum, but she said no.

Never one to let a little 'no' stop me, I became fixated on getting that rabbit. I knew how to address an envelope and get a stamp, and I had seen Mum write her cheques before so my plan was simple – buy the rabbit myself. I took Mum's book and ripped out a blank cheque, then I wrote on it '5 pounds for a rabbit please Peter's Pet Store', and I put it in the envelope and addressed it to 'Peter's Pet Store in Woodingdean'. It must have got there because the next thing I knew, my mum was shouting at me about stealing. The owner – I am guessing Peter – rang my mum and foiled my plan. I never did get that rabbit. I did get another one though but not for a few years later when she had forgiven me. I still don't know why she didn't buy me that rabbit, she knew I would have looked after it because I had recently brought home a small bird that I had found that had fallen from its nest. I brought it in the house and I asked Mum to buy some bird food so I could feed it and keep it alive.

The rabbit I eventually got was called Star. They always say your porn name would be your first pet's name and your mum's maiden name and mum's maiden name was Charlier so my porn name would be Star Charlier. I quite like it, don't you?

'JJ, what do you think?'

He's just given me a look.

If I had the chance to go back in time, instead of calling myself Jordan, I would definitely change my name to Star Charlier. It sounds so showbiz, doesn't it? 'Welcome on stage, Star Charlier!'

Anyway, those were my first pets. I have always been into animals and babies, and nurturing and cuddling. I love it. At the same house, my mum's friend and their daughter, Lisa, had a horse called Echo and it was 12.2 HH (hands heigh, the measurement scale for horses).

It was a grey and quite old but I started riding it and taking it to shows. It was such a naughty little shit. It used to bomb off when I would get on and I would fall off it all the time. But Echo could have thrown me off every single time I got in the saddle and I would not have been deterred – from that point on I absolutely loved horses and still do. My mum found a horse on loan for me and I kept it at a stables called Standean Farm and I would walk or cycle to that place whenever I could. There was a horse there – ironically called 'Star'! – and he was 18 years old and a 14 HH hairy New Forest pony and I absolutely adored him. I could not get enough of that horse. There was a boy at the same stables called Johnny who was a year older than me with freckles all over his face and who had a black horse called Gay that was 13.2 HH. Johnny's mum would sometimes pick me and him up from school and drop us off at the yard and we'd spend hours there. We'd go out on hacks and make up our own show jumps and I loved it. I wonder what he's doing now and whether he remembers me? I used to love going to the bottom of the field to get my horse, have the head collar on him, tie the lead rope around his neck and just gallop him up the hill bareback. It was the best feeling in the world. It makes me so happy that Bunny loves riding too. I bought Junior a pony when he was younger and now Bunny has started riding it and she told me it's the best thing she's ever done. I have just got her her own pony and I know she's out there this minute, mucking out and giving her a brush. She came into the kitchen earlier with her jodhpurs on and her hair all over the place and her mucky boots on, telling me I needed to order a new head collar for her new horse. She would be on my phone ordering it right now and God knows whatever else if I let her. Chip off the old block perhaps?

In the Priory, they told me something that I already knew, but when someone else says it, it gives you some validation – horses, they said, were my safe space. When I kiss the muzzle of a horse and they blow out that air from their nose, that smell to me is 'safety'. Horses are my friends. They don't let me down, they don't cheat on me, they don't write lies about me – they just take me for who I am. When I was younger, they were my friends. I'd spend hours mucking them out, cutting their carrots up and sorting out their feed. Being with them was just the best thing in the world. When it was cold, you'd put your hands under their rugs and it would be so warm and comforting. I hate being cold – even now – and that warmth was the best feeling ever, especially when you couldn't feel your hands after taking the wheelbarrow to the muck heap.

When we went on holiday to Spain as a family when I was younger, I remember there was this horse place you could visit and when we went there were loads of puppies just wandering around too. I desperately wanted one to look after and I brought one back to the villa and said, 'Look, Mum! Can we have it, please?!' She made me take it back. I remember being so upset about that.

Whatever happens in my life I feel that horses are the one thing I can still 'do'. Which is why, when the shitty stories come out about me, and how I've let them run out onto the road and be killed, they don't just piss me off, they really upset me.

Now it's time to set the record straight. According to one particular news story, the RSPCA had been called to my house because one of my horses had collapsed and I had just left it in the field. Of course, they had to come to my house when accusations like that are made concerning animal welfare and there just so happened to be a paparazzi on hand too to take pictures of them coming to my home. I was as confused as they were when they told me about the collapsed horse so we went out to the stables and paddock where the horses were so they could see them all. Then I realised that there was one other horse that they hadn't seen, a metal statue which had fallen into a bit of disrepair and was propped up by one of my oak trees at a bizarre angle. The horse that had 'collapsed' and I was ignoring was in fact my metal horse statue, which had been knocked over and needed fixing in place again. I remember one of the inspectors looking at this horse and saying, 'Tell us this is the horse that was reported,' and I was like, 'Yep!' They found it funny. And it would be funny if it wasn't so fucking ridiculous but there you go. The RSPCA realised it was a complete waste of their time but spent the morning meeting my other animals and dogs and horses (that weren't made from metal) and concluded that everything was OK. They had no concerns, no advice, no recommendations, nothing. They were happy. But that doesn't make a good story for the press, does it? 'Katie Price's animals are looked after and loved'. Who cares?

I have experienced some shocking and heartbreaking situations involving my animals though. I was away filming *Haunted, Live* when I got a call from Kieran saying that my dog, Queenie, had been run over by a Domino's pizza delivery driver on the way out from my house. I couldn't believe it, the driver didn't stop either and I was absolutely in bits when Kieran rang because she was such a good dog. The absolute best dog ever. All the papers reported that I let my German Shepherd run out into the road and be killed. No, my dog was run over on my drive, not because she had been let out to play on a dual carriageway for fuck's sake.

The next thing I know, I had a horse that had escaped and been killed on the road because apparently, I didn't take care of them, or shut the gate properly. In actual fact, I had loaned one of my horses, a black one called Princess, to someone. It was while we were doing the *Pony Club* TV show and I was sitting there watching TV and the doorbell went and it was the police. The road adjacent to where I live is a busy dual carriageway that had been shut off for three hours because some horses had escaped and were running on the road. My first thought was panic, thinking, 'Fuck, is it my horse?' so I went to check all my horses and it wasn't. The police needed some head collars for the escaped horses so I gave them some and I followed them out to the road to see if I could help. That's when I saw my horse dead on the road. It was the horse I had loaned out. I was devastated and I felt so helpless at that point, seeing your horse dead on the road. . . I couldn't get that image out of my head for a very long time. It took me right back to Argentina, when I was in a car crash with my ex-boyfriend Leo, when two wild horses came out of nowhere and hit our jeep. We'd been out quad-biking the whole day and were travelling back to our base on some old beaten track in the dark. I was in the front and the film crew and one of Leo's friends were in the back and all I remember is someone suddenly shouting 'Stop!' and the jeep coming to a complete halt with a shattered front windscreen being inches from my face. It was the most terrifying and traumatic experience I've ever had involving horses and I was so upset.

We all got out of the car and you could hear these horrible noises coming from one horse, who was gasping for breath and horrifically injured. Its back where it hit the car was damaged and I just kept stroking it until it died. We heard the rustling of the other horse who was younger in the ditch next to the road. It was trying to move and was panicking and kept trying to get up but it had also been hit from behind and so its back legs and everything was just. . . it was horrible. I sat there and stroked it and stroked it until it also died in my arms. I will always remember that, the whites of that horse's eyes as it died. Though our car was absolutely fucked, we had no injuries whatsoever, it was a miracle in a way. That memory came flooding back to me as soon as I saw my horse lying there still, and if that upset wasn't great enough, I then read online and in the papers that my horse had been killed on the road because I had left a gate open. It was all my fault apparently, even though the horse wasn't in my care.

At my last house in Ashtead before we moved to West Sussex, I remember we had got Princess a dog. I was upstairs packing for a holiday when I could hear this commotion downstairs and someone shouting, 'Kate! Kate! You've got to come down. . . the dog. . . the dog, it's dead, it's dead!' And I'm like, 'What do you mean, it's dead?!' The breeder we had bought the dog from had given us CBD oil to give this dog and I don't know if Princess had given it too much or what, but we knew it would sleep a lot, and that day it had gone under the reclining chair to sleep and no one had realised and it had been crushed. We took it to the vet's when it died and paid for an autopsy because we wanted to understand what happened and they said the breeder should never have given us CBD to use. Of course, all that was reported was that I had killed Princess's dog because I had a big party and wasn't taking care of it.

The Mucky Mansion, my home now, has been a place of many animals but hand on heart, I think it's cursed. I feel it's cursed with relationships, dramas, bankruptcy and animals. . . all the bad seems to stem from this house.

I'd love to get rid of this house and rent a nice little home somewhere. One thing I do know is that this house has brought me nothing but bad luck and even if I won the lottery, I wouldn't live here. The way I look at it is that I have a roof over my head, so I tell myself not to worry and to enjoy what I have. I sometimes wonder where I would move to if I could. I don't need a bigger house or bit of land, this is 14 acres and that's quite big. I would probably want a smaller, more modern house. Maybe an indoor pool again, like I had at the old house. Everyone loved my indoor pool. Plus, a sauna and a steam room and a *Love Island* garden. Princess says that sounds good and so that sounds good to me too.

My long driveway onto a main road plus my 14 acres of land has been the source of a lot of upset with my animals. There have been times when I've asked someone to come over and feed the dogs if I've been out and I always, always tell them to check the doors are shut and locked when they leave. So one day I was shocked to find out from Facebook that Princess's dog Sparkle had been killed on the road. The whole of social media knew before I was told and I was slammed in the media for not paying attention to my animals when I wasn't there although I had explicitly given careful instructions for this very reason. But the press stories blamed me again.

Unfortunately when one of my animals becomes ill and we have to call the vets, it just gets noted down as another mark in the 'Katie kills her pets' tally chart. I was devasted when one of my horses, Otto, ended up being put down but I knew it was the right thing to do because the vet said he was very ill. I don't neglect any of my animals' needs and I took the advice of the vet, however heartbreaking that was, because when you are a pet owner you can't be selfish and your last great act of kindness is to help your animals and not let them suffer.

I have just uploaded a wonderful video of my cat Frog

and dog Lady playing together – I could watch them for hours playing. Of course I got abuse for that, saying I was letting my dog maul my cat. They were just playing! Frog is so naughty though, he got in the bath with me last night, which was hilarious. I probably shouldn't say that. I'm sure people will now tell me off for that, won't they, Frog? He's just come to sit on my shoulder, which is one of his favourite spots. Although he does like to follow JJ around so if he comes in the kitchen that will be it, he'll scarper after him, won't you, Frog? He turns to look at me then follows JJ out the room. Told you.

A few weeks later after writing this chapter, we noticed that Frog stopped jumping on the side of the kitchen. Then he couldn't jump on the sofa. Then he couldn't jump up on the bed. There was something wrong with him so I took him to the vets. He had a neurological disease. There was absolutely nothing I could do. Within days, it had spread throughout his body to the point that he couldn't even go the toilet on his own. The vet said, there's nothing they could do. So I cuddled him in my arms and he had to be put to sleep. He was only five months old.

CHAPTER 14

JJ

> '**BECAUSE SOMETIMES YOU MEET SOMEONE AND YOU DON'T KNOW HOW OR WHY OR WHAT BROUGHT YOU TOGETHER BUT EVERYTHING FEELS LIGHTER AND BRIGHTER AND BETTER WITH THEM THERE.**'
>
> *Wordporn*

For probably the last 30 years or more, I needed a man. I needed someone in my life. I needed to be loved. I accept that, and I now understand why I would jump from one boyfriend to another, from one relationship to another, from one marriage to another. But now things are different. I don't need a man anymore, I want a man in my life and that's the difference.

I love the conspiracy theories that are out there about me and JJ. I know I shouldn't care but they do make me laugh. Had we been an item before he went on the show?

Are we getting married? Am I moving to Scotland or Yorkshire with him? It's pretty endless. I am afraid to say that how we met, and our lives, are a lot more normal than is made out. We go to the gym and train together, we watch telly in bed together. . . it's all very normal.

What the hell is *MAFS?* My friends had been telling me since October to start watching this TV show (*Married At First Sight*) but I didn't have a clue what it was. I like *Love Island* and they told me it was a bit like that so around Christmas time, I gave it a go. They told me there was a UK version and an Australian version but I had no idea there were so many series.

'Fucking hell, do I need to start from series 1?' That was my first thought. My mind always needs to go to the start of something, to the beginning – I think it's an ADHD thing but that's what I do. 'No, no, you don't need to bother' was the reply and then came the explanation that it's the same concept each series: you get love experts who match people with the attributes they are looking for. Two episodes in, I was hooked.

As soon as I saw JJ walk on camera I thought to myself, 'Phwoar, he's fit!' The TV showed him to be a bit of a party boy from Essex. He looked like he had a nice house and a nice car. He looked like he had his own stuff going on too, which I liked. Plus, he looked trendy and cool but he wasn't loud, he was quiet and mysterious.

Then I saw the thing that he was marrying. Sorry, then I saw Bianca. I just knew they didn't match up. From what I had seen, he loves an American-cheerleader type girl, a model, and I just thought Bianca and him didn't work.

Because I knew he had dated a model before, I remember thinking, 'Bloody hell, I wonder if he would fancy me?' But then the 'negative me' quickly talked myself out of that: 'Don't be stupid, Kate, why would he fancy you? You're fucking 45 years old and you've got five kids.'

But then the more 'positive me' said; 'Hang on, Kate, you don't look 45, you don't dress like a 45-year-old. You have a personality and you're a fucking real model, not like one of those influencers that call themselves models. They're not fucking models, you've been grafting for 30 years and you've been on more magazine covers than they've got followers.' Ha! check me out, bigging myself up!

I don't know, there was just something about JJ. I kept thinking about him and I loved his mysteriousness. After Bianca came Ella and I thought she was stunning. I thought she had a body to die for and was amazing. I didn't have a clue she was transgender, I just thought, they have to fancy each other when they see each other, and I was right. I could see JJ's eyes light up whenever he saw her and you could tell there was chemistry, and that's when I realised that was his type. He loves the fake tits – so again, my mind was like, 'He'll love me, surely?!'

I watched it all and was obsessed. He was so fit but I didn't think anything more of it.

At that point, I didn't really think anything would happen, but then I saw in the paper a story about him having diabetes and that it was life-changing for him and there was a photo of him and he'd lost two stone or something. I thought he looked even better than he had done on *MAFS*. On the show he looked a bit more. . . podgy.

'Podgy?' JJ's just come in with my cup of tea and isn't happy with 'podgy'. He wants me to change it to 'fluffy'. OK, he looked a bit fluffy on the show but now he looked a lot better, he had slightly longer hair and a bit of a beard going on. I fancied him on the show but I definitely fancied him more now.

'No, Kate, you don't want any more relationships, you're done.' My mind was trying to convince myself that I didn't want to pursue this. Besides, I had decided to have a child on my own at that time. I'd even chosen my donor eggs, I had chosen my sperm. I wanted to continue my journey of being a mother on my own without any man in my life (a bit more on this later). But after reading about his diabetes I decided to message JJ. Nothing crazy, but a message. So I made the first move.

'JJ, do you still have the first message I sent you?' I don't have it anymore, I'm hoping he does. He does.

'You wrote: "Just read about you, stay strong",' he smiles, 'then you put a kiss.'

There you go. Short, sweet and simple. No flirting. Didn't I do well? I wasn't looking for a relationship and I always put kisses on my text messages.

'What did you send me back? I can't remember.'

'I can't find it now, it's all a bit deleted,' he is telling me.

'No, you haven't! Find it! it will be good for the book!' God, I do sound bossy, don't I? I don't care, this will be good to share and I know he's found the messages as he starts reading:

'OK,' I said, '"Thank you so much. Dying at the message I sent you in 2022", and then I put a sweating emoji. You replied, "What message? There are no messages on here. LOL", and then you put a kiss and then you put "send it" with a laughing emoji.'

This is brilliant. I love the fact he has kept all this and I can share it with you all. JJ keeps reading our message exchanges.

'I put, "Ha ha ha, FFS. . . should have kept my mouth shut", and I put a crying emoji after that. And then I sent the message that I sent you in 2022.'

'And what did that message say?' I can remember it but it's good to hear it again.

'"Really fancy you tbh,"' JJ is smiling at me. 'That's what I sent you in 2022.'

The crazy thing is I never got that text in 2022 – I would have remembered. In my mind, I am still the one who made the first move when I asked him about his diabetes. I remember asking him if he was based in Essex and he asked me if I was too – lots of people think I'm from Essex.

'I'm in West Sussex near Gatwick, funny enough I'm going to Loughton in an hour for lashes then in another part of Essex at 6 for an hour, everyone thinks I'm Essex, LOL.'

'That's what you replied to me,' says JJ, 'and I said, "Oh is it? tbf you sound a little bit posher than Essex (only a little bit). Are you? Could have told me before, could have got a coffee or something."'

I don't need him to re-read any more messages as I know what happened next. I sent him my phone number and we met for coffee later that day. It was fate again, stepping in. It was fate that I was going to Essex on the day we started texting and so meeting up with him seemed like the most natural thing in the world to do.

I remember it was a Sunday and I had my lashes appointment in Loughton and then I had a make-up masterclass in Clacton. On the way to Essex I said to my friend Jeyda, who was with me, 'Oh, by the way, I have arranged to meet someone after my lashes.' Then I had to explain that I had watched *MAFS* and I just started messaging this guy from the show. I was serious when I told Jeyda that I had no plans to be in a relationship and that I had no real idea about why I was meeting him, other than I thought he was fit. But also, why the hell not? It made sense to meet up while I was there. Besides, there wasn't anything in it – I can be friends with men and women.

So I was sitting in this restaurant, I can't remember which one.

'It was Cote,' says JJ.

I've just asked him. I knew he'd remember.

I was sitting there waiting for him because we had got there first and I said to Jeyda, 'Wonder if he's fit in real life?' It definitely wasn't a date in my mind because when you go on a date you dress up and make a bit of an effort. Because I was going for a make-up masterclass, I didn't have any make-up on. I was totally relaxed, I had a star cardigan on and beige combats. Then he walked in and I was like, 'Hiya! This is Jeyda!'

'I wasn't expecting there to be a welcome party,' JJ said. He's just come over to help me.

'Did you think it was a date?'

'No, I was relaxed like you,' he says. 'I remember I had a coat on because it was so cold, and it was a Sunday. I wasn't expecting to see a cat either!'

'You had a little man bag too!' I remind him. 'I liked

that, I thought you were a chav but cool and I love that tracksuit kind of thing. I think I told you that you look so much better in life than you do on the show, didn't I? I think I made you stand up halfway through to see if you were taller than me. You were, which was a relief.

'JJ. . . What did you think of me?' He's stood up to leave the kitchen but I want to share his first reaction to me.

'I thought you were fit. I fancied you,' he says (good answer). 'I was surprised how down to earth you were, to be honest.'

'Were you pleased you asked to meet me?'

'Technically, it was more of a throwaway comment but you were the one that said, "here's my number" and you arranged it!'

'But you were quick on the reply button too!' I remind him.

'Yeah, I was open to it! But it was really nice, really relaxed.'

'And what did you think when you met me? What else?' I love hearing this.

'I thought you were fit, funny, and you had a good energy.'

'Were you nervous meeting me?' This is something that I probably fear more. I have no idea what crap JJ has seen or read about me in the press. What things he thinks I am like and it has stopped relationships before, when people believe what they read and don't want to get to know the real me.

'I wasn't nervous meeting because you were "Katie Price",' he grins, 'I was nervous because I was like, I might fancy you and I wasn't looking for a girlfriend. But I didn't really know what to expect, if I'm honest. I had no idea. I knew who you were obviously, but I hadn't watched much reality TV as I was in America for years. The first time I saw you was when you were in *I'm a Celebrity. . . Get Me Out Of Here!* I hadn't followed anything after that. I saw you a few times in the papers and stuff but that's it. I was nervous, as I would have been meeting anyone I fancied.'

He's good, isn't he? I remember I didn't want to leave. I wanted to stay another five minutes and then another five minutes. It was the first time I didn't feel suffocated. I thought there was something about him and I definitely fancied him. We only had 45 minutes to make it work but we did. We had a nice chat and I know he was a little nervous when he came in. When Jeyda said, 'We've got to go,' I didn't want to leave.

'I think we kissed on the lips when we said "bye",' I say. 'Did we?'

'I remember,' I tell him, and I can. I went off to my make-up masterclass and as soon as it was finished, we started messaging and we continued for my whole journey home. Then when I got home, I called him and we chatted on the phone for hours.

I knew I wanted to see him again but I was also telling myself, 'Kate, no.' No relationships. I was so exhausted with them. Still, I asked him what he was doing the next day, and in another twist of fate, he told me he was going to the *Geordie Shore* premiere. I had also been invited and was going with my friends. When I found out he was going to be there my tummy started doing some excited flips.

We arranged to meet up with our friends before the premiere and then we all went out together afterwards. Eventually we went back to a hotel and my friend Chloe was in the bed next to me on one side and JJ was on the other side. We were just chatting away to each other. Of course, I was trying to have a little feel-up but he had all his clothes on! So I sort of rolled my elbow over his crotch, thinking, 'What's it like, I wonder?!' I couldn't help it!

But I was still confused. I knew I fancied him but I kept saying to myself, 'No! Don't go there, Kate!'

Then he left for the night. We carried on messaging after that, it was so easy to message him. I don't even think it was flirty. He had made it clear he wasn't looking for a girlfriend, having come straight from *MAFS*, which he said was quite intense. I kept thinking of how much I wanted to see him again even though I wasn't looking for anything serious either. I was so drawn to him. He wasn't the normal, beggy type man who would say, 'I want to see you again, I want to fuck you.' That is a real ICK for me, he wasn't anything like that. He was so hard to work out and in the end I wanted to shake him and say, 'Can you just tell me if you fancy me or something!' I felt like a teenager. He did fancy me, and I fancied him.

I wasn't looking for someone but these things have a way of working out when you least expect it. Will this be forever? Who knows. What I do know is that he makes me happy and excited when I think about him. I get no aggravation from him and we are taking things slowly, and I have never done it slowly! I won't rush things because of the kids but they have gotten to know him and they like him. They also know I'd been speaking to him for a long time before they met him properly.

We all went bowling together, there was a group of six of us and that was fun. Then we went rollerblading the following week so they associate him with having fun and me being happy. I couldn't believe it when the social worker who came in asked me if he was DBS checked. She had seen him on *MAFS* and thought that he needed to have some sort of criminal records check. I'm not going to bring any random man home to meet my children and I will not be dictated to by social workers. What business is it of theirs? You think I'm going to ask a guy I meet, 'Hello, do you have a DBS check?' How degrading is that?

Just another example of someone thinking that they can control me.

I like the fact that JJ has been on a TV show and understands the industry a little bit. He lived out in America for a while on a scholarship, playing football out there while he studied for a degree in Psychology. He's been to celeb parties in expensive houses and he's just not bothered by it at all. He's 32 this year and there will be the same age gap between me and him as there is with my mum and Paul. So, Mum can't moan about that. It works for me, that he's younger. He's calm and so kind. I am the third girlfriend he's ever had so that's a massive thing for him. Being in a relationship is a big deal. I also know he's not easy to get, which I like – The Challenge! Ha! But I got there.

CHAPTER 15

IVF

'AND SOMETIMES AGAINST ALL ODDS, AGAINST ALL LOGIC, WE STILL HOPE.'

Reproductive care centre

I am going to have another baby. There is a clinic that currently has some donor eggs and sperm ready and is waiting for me to come in and have them implanted. I went through a list of suitable donors and I have chosen sperm from a man who is mixed race from America and although I potentially have one egg that would be viable, I have chosen to have a donor egg too. I can categorically say – I will be having a baby.

I am 46 years old and people don't understand why I want more children. They will say things like, 'Kate, your kids are a bit older now, you can start enjoying your life more!', and my reaction is always the same: 'No, I want more kids, my life is my kids.' It doesn't matter what job

I am doing, or where I am, my kids come first. They are always with me.

Other friends then talk to me about the menopause and ask am I worried about going through it? Absolutely not! I am still having periods but if it comes to a point when I am too old and I can't carry a baby, there is always a surrogate. Either way, I am having a baby. I would buy one from aboard if I could. That's how sure I am about all of this. There is absolutely no way I am not having more babies. I don't care what people say, it's my life. I want more children and I am not done.

Yes, I probably would be devastated if I couldn't carry another child myself, but as I say, I would then use a surrogate, and even if it's not biologically mine, I would love it with all my heart.

I have always been a nurturing type. As a child if I saw a bird fall from a nest or a wild rabbit alone or anything like that, I'd want to bring it in and look after it and keep it. I have always loved dolls and prams. I had a cat when I was younger and I would push it around in a pram and put clothes on it. Poor Bernard. He was a white cat with one green and one blue eye.

When my mum told me she was pregnant with my sister, I was so excited. We didn't have a lot of money so she bought a second-hand Maclaren Dreamer Buggy, which was mauve and had a shell pattern all over it.

I was obsessed with this buggy. I would push it around and around all day long. I was so excited when my sister was born. I would sometimes pinch her when she was in her cot or when Mum had just put her down, just so she would cry and then I'd have an excuse to pick her up. So growing up, I have always known I wanted to have a baby. I have been through the mill with my pregnancies too. I have been kicked in the stomach and lost a baby, had several miscarriages, had failed IVFs, I've had ectopic pregnancies too. I have also had abortions. I went into the clinic to abort Harvey three times but in the end I couldn't go through with it.

I sat there in the surgical gown that they give you, on my own and ready to have my Marmite sandwich afterwards (they always give you a Marmite sandwich) and I couldn't think of one good reason to get rid of my baby. It just hit me as I sat there. I thought to myself, 'Why? Why am I getting rid of it?' So I decided to keep him. I have talked lots about this before so I won't go into the details now but it was, from that moment on, the most perfect pregnancy.

I was living my best life at that moment too. Being pregnant didn't stop me going out. I still went clubbing, going out to Chinawhite and having fun. I'd be wearing all my party gear, my little skirts and my little top. The paps were always there, trying to get a photo of me coming out of the club looking bleary-eyed. They took so many photos there was bound to be one of me blinking and that was the photo they used. They stopped taking photos when I got round the corner and found my car because I was the designated driver taking everyone else home. But 'pregnant women comes out of club sober' isn't a story.

Harvey's pregnancy was the best and he is the best kid – well, he's a man now. It was always me and him against the world. There was no aggro or stress from anyone else because his dad, Dwight, didn't want anything to do with him so it was me in control. All the other pregnancies and births have all been different in that sense and I'm convinced that's why they weren't plain sailing. So I'm not afraid of having a child by myself again, in my mind it would be a lot less stress and I would be a lot happier. JJ is only young though but he knows everything there is to know about me, including my desire to have more children. I don't want to put any pressure on him. He would rather he fathered my child than use a donor, but we've not quite had a chance to talk about it all properly. All I know is that having Harvey was the best decision I ever made.

But fucking hell, did his birth hurt!

I had no epidural, and he was 8lb 13oz. All I had was gas and air and they had to induce me and use two of those fucking hooks to break my waters. Thinking about it, it would be quite therapeutic to give an overview of everything that happened in all of my pregnancies and births, so here goes. . .

I remember being so paranoid about the nurses seeing me with my legs open. I remember I didn't want to get my hair wet as I was getting in and out of the bath. Oh, and the pessaries they put in, fucking hell! I had Harvey while I was squatting and I remember that's when the werewolf in me came out. I have never made a noise like it! I have never, ever heard noises like that come out from my body.

I did a playlist of music during labour, but when the contractions started it got to the point where I couldn't fucking bear the pain and I had to have complete silence. I could hear my mum and my friend whispering to each other and I kept shouting to them to stop because I couldn't concentrate. I genuinely don't know how I didn't break their hands as I held them so tightly because fucking hell, it was horrific. I don't care what anyone says: you can go to any antenatal class in the world, you can have all the meditation bollocks you want if you think that will help you be calm, but giving birth is fucking painful. That baby is coming out of your body one way or another and it will hurt regardless of the music you play, or the chanting you do, or the soothing breathing you try. Giving birth scared the shit out of me, it genuinely frightened me to death. But then holding Harvey afterwards. . . I didn't want to let him go.

Having Harvey was the best decision I ever made. He came everywhere with me and I was very protective over who held him. I wouldn't let other people near him, only my mum or a few close friends. I was the same with all my children. I couldn't stand it when certain then 'relatives' held some of my babies. Fuck me, I hated that. I can't explain why, but it was like I was giving away a part of me every time I let someone hold my baby and I hated it.

The door is always open for Dwight to make contact with Harvey. Always. I would absolutely love Dwight to meet him, because he is just the absolute best. He is so funny and has such a personality. It makes me so sad and I genuinely don't know what it is with Dwight. If I knew there was a charity event that he was going to, I would deliberately turn up with Harvey. He would then be forced to meet him and I think if that ever happened, his mind would change forever. I think if he ever got in touch, he would want to see him all the time after that. Harvey is such a polite young man and I know Dwight would be proud of his son. He never asks about his dad, he doesn't understand. If you ask Harvey who Dwight is, he will just say, 'He's black,' that's all. The strangest times for me are when Harvey is here and there is a soft football in the kitchen and he will give it a little tap, a little kick with his foot. I stop and think, 'Isn't it strange to think that his dad was an amazing footballer?' It's mad. Harvey has absolutely no idea.

Junior's pregnancy was completely different. I was so sick and I had such bad sciatica. I had him two weeks early in the end. I was booked in for a C-section at the Portland Hospital. I was getting pressure from people to have him naturally and to breastfeed and my reaction then is the same as it is now: 'Fuck off. Let me do things my own way.' No baby is going to suck on my bitty bitty, and they haven't! I believe it's all choice and new mothers should not, under any circumstances, feel the pressure to do something or not do something because of what someone else says. When you are a mother you have to do what works best for you. I certainly wasn't going to be vilified for choosing to bottle feed when millions of women over the world do it.

With Princess I was sick again, and again had really bad sciatica. I always used to bath in Decléor oil and to this day, I don't have one stretch mark on my body. I even oiled my minge, don't ask me why. Am I weird for doing that? I am sure other people do it. It helped me feel good. When I went in for my C-section with Princess I was bald, shaven clean, my hair and my nails were all done. I like to look after myself.

Out of all the pregnancies, Jett was probably the worst. Not only did I feel awful and put on nearly four stone with him, it was during my pregnancy with Jett that Kieran started an affair, so I don't have any good memories of that time.

Jett was born in France and had to be in an incubator for six weeks until we could take him home so it was a stressful time.

Bunny's pregnancy was the most stressful because that was when I found out Kieran was at it again and had started cheating when I was about four or five months pregnant. It was a scary pregnancy in so many ways. My waters were about to break at 22 weeks so I had to have an emergency cervical stitch. The doctors wanted me to try and get to 28 weeks when there was more chance of survival and in the end Bunny was born at 31 weeks. Both Jett and Bunny were premature and I was so stressed. It was so awful. What should have been the most amazing time was blighted because of the trauma of what I was going through. So do I want another baby as some sort of closure to my horrific pregnancies? To prove to myself that I can have a pregnancy that isn't stressful or traumatic? I don't think like that at all. In fact, as soon as Bunny was born, I said 'I want another' right after she came out. Is it a coping mechanism? A way to block out the pain of the trauma and the chaos around me? I don't know. Maybe.

I underwent IVF before I had Jett and Bunny, but knowing what I know now, I am pleased those times weren't successful. With Kieran I fell pregnant naturally but after having Bunny and getting with Carl, I haven't been able to conceive naturally. Carl and I went through rounds of IVF and I did fall pregnant, but I miscarried quite early on. That was fate too. But having failed IVF and then having IVF only to miscarry is very horrific. There are so many women like me out there who are struggling to conceive and yet we don't talk about it as much as we should. Women go through so much when it comes to getting pregnant and not only is there an incredible strain physically on your body when it happens, emotionally when it doesn't happen it can really fuck with your mind. You start to doubt your body and what it can do. Which is why, if needs be, I won't be the one carrying my next baby if my body isn't up to it. I have no issue with having a surrogate. You can see why I say I'm pretty determined to have a child – nothing is going to stop me having a baby.

CHAPTER 16

TO BE CONTINUED...

'IN A WORLD WHERE YOU CAN BE ANYTHING, BE KIND.'

Caroline Flack

would like to say this final chapter signals an end to all my drama, but you know me, there is never an end to it! Kerry's quote about my life being something Spielberg couldn't make up still makes me laugh. I am in talks to do the TV show *Banged Up*, which will be right up my street. They were telling me that I would be in a maximum-security women's prison with some real tough characters, murderers and all sorts, and I was like, 'Brilliant! Bring it on!' Everyone has been trying to put me behind bars for years, I might as well put myself there first! I am also doing my MisFits boxing, a crossover boxing promotion by YouTuber KSI, and they are training me up. I had to have a brain scan and a body scan and sign a contract. I did ask the man who was doing all the tests if I am the oldest person coming for boxing and he said, 'Yeah', but then he paused before saying, 'But you're in good nick for your age!' Ha! That made me chuckle.

I am in good nick for my age! I think I'm fighting someone a lot younger but it's OK. I'm in good shape for an old lady. Ha! See, there is still entertainment coming from me.

I can't wait for all my singing gigs and to release a single. How funny that Eurovision has been the biggest regret of my career and now I'm back singing. But I am doing it my way this time. Doing the songs I want to do, songs that mean something. I will also be doing music festivals and doing a tour. I want to give people goosebumps when they hear me. You can't hide your voice when you are singing those powerful ballads and I can't wait. I want to own that stage and make people sit back in shock – she can actually sing! I get slated all the time for singing but I love it. I love performing in the studio too – it's something so special, when it's just you and the mic. When you hear yourself back and all the sound is echoing, it's amazing. The good thing is that you can now release songs on your own terms, your own way, and you can send them everywhere, you don't need people doing it for you.

I hope you've been able to take a breath while reading this book. You will probably agree with my statement that men have been the main problem in my life, that they have been my downfall and the cause of all my stress and heartache. Having read it, you can't say I'm not a survivor though and you can't accuse me of being anything but honest about my experiences and feelings. These are my memories, these are my truths. I know I have a meme about me that says, 'This happened, then this happened, then this happened, then this happened. . .' I get it. I hear myself recalling all this drama, and all these stories, and I think to myself, 'Fucking hell, Kate, how much shit can one person have in their life?'

Perhaps that should be my next book – a self-help one on how to overcome trauma? I could probably do a guide-book on all sorts of things – bankruptcy, what to do when your partner cheats, child abuse, PTSD, ADHD. You can't tell me that there is a person in this industry who has dealt with the same level of shit I have and is still here, smiling, trying to be positive and wanting to tell the tale? Can you think of anyone? I can't. I do enjoy my life, I do enjoy being able to do my podcast and tell the world what's happening in my own words. I love my children and I love being a mum. I do need to have words with Junior though – he's a man now and is growing up fast, and is in a relationship too. . . I guess he will have to learn his lessons the hard way, like I did. Princess is happy and Bunny is out with her horse, so I know she's loving life. Harvey sent me a video of himself on the keyboard, which I play all the time when I miss him, and Jett is looking forward to starting his new school in September. So there are lots of things that I am grateful for and that is a good focus for me.

Such is the life of Katie Price, I know that by the time you buy this book and read it, there will have been lots of new drama and chaos that I've had to deal with, but don't worry, I will keep notes and then you can have another book to read another time. There is a quote from a famous actress that says you should always leave your audience wanting more and you can guarantee there will always be more to tell in the near future. Will I stay in my house or be made homeless? Will my bankruptcy disputes be resolved? Will JJ and I start a family? Will I finally be happy with how I look? Too many questions to answer. So for now, let's just leave it with this: to be continued. . .

EPILOGUE

I am writing this chapter with seven days left to leave my house. By the time you read this I will have been evicted after having just two weeks' notice and I will be living somewhere new and you know what? I can't. Fucking. Wait.

But my God, I have so many boxes to pack. I have everyone coming over later and they are helping me pack. We've packed away the kids' rooms and my dressing room but a house this size, to get everything packed and shipped out in under two weeks? It's a fucking joke.

So for the past few weeks I've been working like mad to find a new place, to find a new home for the kids and to be able to send all my belongings to. And you know what? When you read this, I will be in my new house and

I fucking love it!. You can't ever say that I don't like to keep you up to date with what's happening!

At the time of writing this I am still unsure what the plan is or what will happen with it all, but I'm getting through it.

I would also love to think that the press will now get off my back, will now understand everything that I've been dealing with so far, why my life has been so hard and why the stories they've been writing about me this year are untrue. My bankruptcy situation started when I was unwell, when I had a breakdown and when ignoring everything was far easier than confronting it. The 'well' me sees that isn't right and that isn't the way to deal with problems but the unwell me at the time said it was the only way to live, to shut everything out. But I'm engaging with it all now and in a much happier place.

Did I tell you that when I was having my breakdown, my real dad, Ray and his wife, Sher moved in with me to keep an eye on me? It really helped me at a time I thought nothing would. I had long chats with my dad and, despite what has happened in our lives and that he has not been a huge part of it for so long, when I was at my lowest, he was there. Perhaps there is something to say for that, I don't know. I haven't quite analysed it more than the fact that when I hit rock bottom, he appeared. And he came to help me when I needed him the most.

What more can I say? I loved it. I loved having him there looking after me and he was so supportive. It was a bit surreal. I was like, 'my dad is here, my biological dad. . . and he's helping me.' He stayed with me for quite a while and I won't ever forget it.

Right. . . I need to get on. I need to make some tea for the people who've come in to help me pack everything up. I was going to offer to do everyone a roast dinner but that's too much work for me when I should be packing. Maybe I'll just order pizza instead. I can't wait to be in my new home now.

It's a house that I realise now I have always wanted. A brand-new build, a smaller house, a peaceful house, no ghosts, no awful memories. This house has nothing but bad energy for me now. You'll have to wait for the next book to find out more about that.

This is a new chapter for me and in the space of writing this book, everything in my world has changed and I can't tell you how excited I am about that. I am thinking of it as a fresh start. Everything is there on my doorstep and it's a dream come true for me.

I'm looking round at all the stuff I need gone and rather than it stress me out, I'm thinking that this has been exactly what I needed – to make me confront everything and sort a lot of my issues out. I have found that process hugely satisfying. I suppose because it hasn't been a choice of mine, because I have had to confront it and I have had to deal with it and getting rid of stuff has been very cleansing. I've been ruthless with the stuff I have got rid of but it's done me the world of good. I think that's probably quite normal too, isn't it? When you finally have a sort-out of all the material stuff you have, it shows what really matters in life.

And maybe I am quite refreshing to some people, maybe me going through something like this helps other people who might think it's the end of the world. It's really not. I'm still earning money, I'm still working and so I hope I inspire people in a strange way. I hope they look at me and go, 'OK, even celebrities go through this shit but Kate deals with it and she's OK.'

I want people to know that I've hit rock bottom. No one knows what goes on when someone is feeling suicidal. I had the full force of the UK media deal with my breakdown, my illness, my misfortune. But I'm coming back up. This might seem a strange place to leave things as there is still so much I want to share with you all. . . But I suppose you'll just have to wait until my next book to hear about that. . .

ACKNOWLEDGEMENTS

This book has taken me back 30 years in time and there are a few people I would like to thank for being with me every step of that journey.

My family are the team who always have my back, who pick me up when I need them and who surround me with love – even when I don't ask for it or when I don't realise how much I am in need of it. So, I want to say a big thank you to my mum, my dad Paul, my biological dad Ray and his wife Sher, my sister Soph, Harry and my brother Dan.

Special thanks to Abi Smith for helping me bring my story to the page. My story is punctuated with ugly truths but beautiful comebacks and I hope everyone who reads it may understand me a little better than they did before. Or maybe (hopefully) realise that everything you might have read in the press doesn't show the real me. This is me.

Thank you to my friends Kerry Katona, Ross, Marchello, Lou and Daz and Kalelah, Jeyda, Fern and Ryan.

Last, but never least, I want to thank my five wonderful children: Harvey, Junior, Princess, Jett and Bunny. You are my loves and my life, and you are the reason I am a survivor.

ADDITIONAL RESOURCES

Trust me, I've learned the hard way but it's OK to reach out to ask for help and there's a lot out there. Here's just a few things that helped me and I hope they help you too:

ADHD:
ADHD UK - Homepage - ADHD UK

The Royal College of Psychiatrists website: rcpsych.ac.uk/expertadvice/problems/adhdinadults.aspx

National Attention Deficit Disorder Information Support Service (ADDISS) is a national charity for individuals with ADHD and their families and offers educational resources and information regarding local groups.

AADD-UK is a small charity founded by members in Bristol, London and Newcastle, and is currently running several affiliated support groups as well as an interactive website and online community: aadduk.org

Bankruptcy Advice:
www.gov.uk/bankruptcy
www.citizensadvice.org.uk

Domestic Abuse:
www.victimsupport.org.uk
www.refuge.org.uk
www.rapecrisis.org.uk

Idiopathic Pulmonary Fibrosis information:
www.nhs.co.uk

PTSD:
www.mind.org.uk
www.nhs.uk/mental-health/conditions/post-traumatic-stress-disorder-ptsd/treatment/
www.ptsd.org